GW01149156

EDWARD BOYLE

Edward Boyle
His life by his friends

Edited by
Ann Gold

M
MACMILLAN

© Ann Gold 1991

All rights reserved. No reproduction, copy or transmission of this publication may be made without written permission.

No paragraph of this publication may be reproduced, copied or transmitted save with written permission or in accordance with the provisions of the Copyright, Designs and Patents Act 1988, or under the terms of any licence permitting limited copying issued by the Copyright Licensing Agency, 33–4 Alfred Place, London WC1E 7DP.

Any person who does any unauthorised act in relation to this publication may be liable to criminal prosecution and civil claims for damages.

First published 1991

Published by
MACMILLAN ACADEMIC AND PROFESSIONAL LTD
Houndmills, Basingstoke, Hampshire RG21 2XS
and London
Companies and representatives
throughout the world

Printed in Great Britain by
WBC Print, Bridgend, S. Wales

British Library Cataloguing in Publication Data
Edward Boyle: His Life by his Friends
1. Great Britain. Politics. Boyle, Edward Boyle, Baron, 1923–
I. Gold, Ann, 1926–
941.085'092'4

ISBN 0-333-51028-3

Contents

List of Plates	vii
Preface	viii
Acknowledgements	ix
Notes on the Contributors	xi
1 Introduction *Ann Gold*	1
2 Edward at home *Elizabeth Longford*	48
3 At Preparatory School *Michael Howard*	55
4 Eton and Early Politics *John Grigg*	59
5 Cricket and Race Relations *David Lane*	73
6 The Oxford Union and After *Tony Benn*	81
7 At the Treasury *Robert Neild*	85
8 In the House of Commons *Robert Rhodes James*	91
9 At the Education Ministry: An Official's View *Maurice Kogan*	95
10 At the Education Ministry: His Junior Minister's View *Christopher Chataway*	104
11 A Cabinet Colleague *John Boyd-Carpenter*	113
12 A Supporter of Friends and Causes *Edward Heath*	117

13 The Move Away from Politics *William Rees-Mogg*	120
14 The Vice-Chancellor at Work *Christine Challis*	124
15 The Vice-Chancellor and Student Unrest *Sue Slipman*	135
16 The Vice-Chancellor in Office *William Walsh*	138
17 Guiding the Top Salaries Review Body *Jean Orr*	147
18 Edward as Musician *Alexander Goehr*	155
19 Presiding at the Leeds Piano Competition *Fanny Waterman*	166
20 The Benevolent Uncle *Georgina Dunlop*	174
Index	180

List of Plates

1 Edward Boyle aged seven, with his mother, his brother and sister and their nanny.
2 Aged 12, on a sightseeing visit to Hamburg with his father.
3 At Oxford in 1947, with fellow-officers of the University Conservative Association; on his left, Margaret Roberts (later Mrs Thatcher).
4 In 1948 as President of the Oxford Union with his guest speaker, Lord Balfour of Inchrye.
5 At a garden party in his constituency in the early 1950s. (D. Page, Birmingham)
6 As Minister of Education. (*The Huddersfield Examiner*)
7 As a member of Sir Alec Douglas-Home's Cabinet in 1964. (Crown Copyright, COI)
8 Taking his seat in the House of Lords in 1970, with his supporters, Lord Butler of Saffron Walden and Lord Fulton of Falmer. (The Press Association)
9 As chairman of the 1972 jury of the Leeds Piano Competition, talking to Mlle. Nadia Boulanger. (*The Yorkshire Post*)
10 With the prize-winners of the 1972 Leeds Piano Competition, (l. to r.) Eugene Indjic, Murray Perahia and Craig Sheppard. (*The Yorkshire Post*)
11 Conferring an honorary degree of Leeds University on Mlle. Nadia Boulanger in 1972.
12 As Vice-Chancellor of Leeds University with the Chancellor, H.R.H. The Duchess of Kent, the Pro-Chancellor Sir Richard Graham and the honorary graduates of 1973. (Picturehouse Ltd., Bradford)

Preface

This biography takes a special form, in order to illustrate the particular quality of Edward Boyle's life. He did not hold any of the highest offices; nevertheless, for nearly thirty years he had a gentle but widespread influence on a variety of people in many areas of public life.

An account of his life written by a single person would fail to do full justice to the range and nature of his influence. This biography, therefore, is written by many people. An introductory chapter gives a short but complete factual account of Edward Boyle's life, and is followed by a series of essays written by former colleagues and friends. These are set in a chronological sequence, and they discuss in greater detail certain periods and events of his life to which the introduction has only briefly referred.

Acknowledgements

It is a measure of the respect and affection in which Edward was held that so many busy and distinguished contributors were immediately willing to write for this book. I am deeply grateful to them for their generous response to my original letter, and for their co-operation since.

Among the contributors, John Grigg holds a special place. It was he who proposed the form the book should take, and I am greatly indebted to him for his constant encouragement and wise advice.

As far as my own Introduction is concerned, I am grateful to all those who helped me prepare it. In most cases, their names appear in the text or in the notes, but there are still a few others I would like to mention here.

Maureen Ross was Secretary to the Vice-Chancellor during Edward's time at Leeds: in recording the last decade of his life I have greatly profited from her suggestions and advice, as well as from her patient help in looking for papers.

I am grateful for substantial help from Professor Peter Gosden regarding Edward's thoughts on education while at Leeds. Others who have been especially helpful in providing information for me are Sir Arthur Drew, Lord Goodman, Margaret McCreath, James McGregor, Professor George McNicol, Sir Albert Sloman and John Wilding.

Special thanks are due to Peter Calvocoressi, who discussed the whole idea of the book at the outset, and also to Jim Rose, who, among other help, was instrumental in enabling me to learn for the first time what Edward did during the war.

Sir William van Straubenzee kindly read the complete typescript of the Introduction; I am grateful for similar help from Don Rimmington and Professor Charles Whewell.

Notes on the Contributors

The Rt. Hon. Anthony (Tony) Wedgwood Benn has been a Labour Member of Parliament since 1950. He was Postmaster-General, 1964–66, Minister of Technology, 1966–70, and Secretary of State for Industry, later Secretary of State for Energy, 1974–79. His publications include two volumes of his diaries.

The Rt. Hon. Lord Boyd-Carpenter. John Boyd-Carpenter was called to the Bar in 1934, and was a Conservative Member of Parliament, 1945–72, when he was created a life peer. He was Financial Secretary to the Treasury, 1951–54, Minister of Pensions and National Insurance, 1955–62 and Chief Secretary to the Treasury and Paymaster General, 1962–64.

Christine Challis went to Leeds University as an administrator in 1969 and was appointed Deputy Secretary in 1974. Since 1983 she has been Secretary of the London School of Economics and Political Science.

The Rt. Hon. Christopher Chataway represented Britain in the Olympic Games of 1952 and 1956; in 1954 he held the world 5000 metres record. In 1959 he was elected a Conservative Member of Parliament and was Parliamentary Secretary at the Ministry of Education, 1962–64. He was Minister of Posts and Telecommunications, 1970–72 and Minister for Industry, 1972–74. He then left Parliament to take up the post of Managing Director of Orion Bank. He is now Chairman of Crown Communications Group PLC.

Georgina Dunlop worked for a publisher until the birth of her first child. She is married to Neil Dunlop, a petroleum engineer, and they have two children.

Alexander Goehr was Professor of Music at Leeds University, 1971–76, and has been Professor of Music and Fellow of Trinity Hall, Cambridge, since 1976. In 1980 he was Visiting Professor at the Peking Conservatoire of Music. In 1987 he was the BBC Reith Lecturer.

Notes on the Contributors

John Grigg was editor of the *National and English Review*, 1954–60. He was a columnist for the *Guardian*, 1960-70 and since 1986 he has been with *The Times*. His publications include the first three volumes of a life of Lloyd George. Since 1985 he has been chairman of the London Library.

The Rt. Hon. Edward Heath has been a Conservative Member of Parliament since 1950. He was government Chief Whip, 1955–59, Lord Privy Seal with Foreign Office responsibilities, 1960–63 and Secretary for Trade, Industry and Regional Development and President of the Board of Trade 1963–64. He was Leader of the Opposition, 1965–70, and Prime Minister between 1970 and 1974.

Sir Michael Howard was Professor of War Studies at King's College, London University, 1963–68. He was a Fellow of All Souls' College, Oxford, 1968–80 and Chichele Professor of the History of War, 1977–80. He was a Fellow of Oriel College, Oxford, 1980–89, and Regius Professor of Modern History; then Lovett Professor of Military and Naval History, Yale University, from October 1989.

Maurice Kogan was private secretary to Edward Boyle at the Ministry of Education, 1957–59. Since leaving the Civil Service in 1967 he has specialised in various studies of the politics and organisation of the welfare state. He is the author of many works on educational and higher education policy and on NHS organisation and science policy. He is Professor of Government and Social Administration and Dean of Social Sciences at Brunel University.

Sir David Lane worked in the steel and oil industries after graduating from Cambridge University in 1947. From 1967 to 1976 he was Conservative Member of Parliament for Cambridge. In 1970 he was appointed PPS to Mr (now Lord) Carr, Secretary of State for Employment, and he was a junior Minister at the Home Office, 1972-74. From 1977 to 1982 he served as the first Chairman of the Commission for Racial Equality.

The Countess of Longford. Elizabeth Longford was born in 1906 and is the author of many biographies, including *Victoria RI*, *Wellington*, *Wilfred Scawen Blunt* and *Byron*. She twice stood for Parliament as a Labour candidate. She married Frank Pakenham (now Lord

Longford) and they have had eight children.

Robert Neild served in the economic section, Cabinet Office and Treasury, 1951–56. He was Economic Adviser to the Treasury, 1964–67. From 1967 to 1971 he was Director, Stockholm International Peace Research Institute. From 1971 to 1984 he was Professor of Economics at the University of Cambridge.

Jean Orr served in the Treasury, where she was promoted to Assistant Secretary in 1961. She was lent to the Office of Manpower Economics as Secretary to the Top Salaries Review Body in 1971. She was Director, Office of Manpower Economics, 1973–80.

Lord Rees-Mogg. William Rees-Mogg was City Editor of the *Sunday Times*, 1960–61, Political and Economic Editor 1961–63 and Deputy Editor 1964–67. He was Editor of *The Times*, 1967–81, and Chairman of the Arts Council, 1982–89. In 1988 he was created a life peer and appointed Chairman of the Broadcasting Standards Council.

Robert Rhodes James was Assistant Clerk, House of Commons, 1955–61 and Senior Clerk 1961–64. He was elected Conservative Member of Parliament for Cambridge in 1976. He is a Fellow of All Souls' College, Oxford, and among his many publications are *Rosebery* (1963) and *Anthony Eden* (1986).

Sue Slipman was Secretary and National President of the National Union of Students, 1975–78. She was Area Officer, National Union of Public Employees, 1975–85, and Chair, Women for Social Democracy, 1983–86. Since 1985 she has been Director of the National Council for One Parent Families.

William Walsh was Professor of Education, University of Leeds, 1957–72; he was Professor of Commonwealth Literature, University of Leeds, 1972–84. He was Pro-Vice-Chancellor from 1965 to 1967 and Acting Vice-Chancellor from 1981 to 1983. Among his many publications are *FR Leavis* (1981), *Higher Education; pattern of change in the 1970s* (1972) and *Introduction to Keats* (1981).

Fanny Waterman studied the piano with Tobias Matthay and later with Cyril Smith. Despite her successful career as a performer, she decided to turn to teaching. In 1963 she was joint founder with

Marion Harewood of the Leeds International Pianoforte Competition, of which she is now the Chairman of the Jury. She has given master-classes all over the world and is the author of several books on piano playing.

1

Introduction

Ann Gold

FAMILY AND CHILDHOOD, 1923–33

Edward Charles Gurney Boyle was born on 31 August 1923 in London, at 63 Queen's Gate in South Kensington. His grandparents had bought the house in 1891 and after his grandfather's death in 1909 Edward's father and grandmother continued to live there. His father loved the house, saying that the broad, plane-tree-lined Queen's Gate was the only real 'boulevard' in London and that the outlook towards the gardens of the Natural History Museum was exceptionally spacious and agreeable. When Edward's father married in 1920 and looked for a new home for his mother, it happened by chance that the next door house, No. 64, became vacant, and so she moved in there. Edward's grandmother played quite an active part in his life until the war, because she was interested in children and fond of amusing them. She also had abundant energy and plenty of time to spare, so that whenever Edward's parents were away from home – which was quite often – she felt justified in participating in her grandchildren's lives even more than usual. The two houses had a communicating passage on the nursery floor and the grandmother's house had a passenger lift, which Edward's nanny used rather than carry a child up 72 stairs in his own home.

Michael Jaffé remembers those days:

> Edward Boyle's parents and his father's mother had adjacent, intercommunicating houses in Queen's Gate a few yards from Wagner's, the first of the schools which he and I attended together. Old Lady Boyle, who had her own views on a range of subjects from Shakespeare to Serbia, liked to meet her grandson's friends.
>
> She and a bust of Mr Gladstone were unforgettable presences to which domestic reverence was due. Before I left this double mansion after my first tea with Edward, he put a jigsaw puzzle into

my hands, a map of Ireland. I was overcome by this first present from anyone outside my immediate family and godparents. 'My grandmother told me to be kind to you,' he said.[1]

Edward's grandfather[2] and father[3] were both distinguished in their own fields, but their interests and their personalities were quite different. His grandfather, born in 1848, was intended for the Army, but his father's early death forced him instead to leave school at 16 and find employment. He was immensely hard-working and made a success in two careers: first, as a surveyor, when he diligently worked his way up in the profession, becoming a specialist in the value of urban land at a time when London was expanding very fast. At the age of 40, however, he decided to become a barrister. He went to a 'crammer' to study for the law examinations, and had to learn Latin from the very beginning. His fellow-students were nearly 20 years younger than he, but he surprised them all by his good memory and his powers of mental arithmetic. When called to the Bar he made use of his special knowledge of the value of property, and became an expert in problems of local taxation and land values. He wrote a book on rating, which was the best book of its kind at the time.

He was widely respected for the shrewdness of his judgement on such matters as the amalgamation of the London docks and the need for a Port of London Authority. He became a KC and in 1904 he was made a baronet on the recommendation of Arthur Balfour. He fought unsuccessfully two parliamentary elections on behalf of the Conservative Party at Hastings and at Rye, before being elected for the division of Taunton in 1906.

Constantly in demand for his professional skills and discerning advice, he worked increasingly hard: he earned high fees and enjoyed his success but by the time he was elected to Parliament he had already over-taxed his strength. In 1905 he went to Singapore to help arbitrate the purchase price of the docks being bought by the British Government; while there he suffered severely from the heat and the hearings were adjourned more than once due to his illness. He was already 57 when he became an MP and he died at 60, retaining nearly to the end his exceptional memory and mental agility with figures.

Edward's father, born in 1878, led a quite different life, and did not have the same urge for hard work; on the contrary, he particularly enjoyed having the leisure to travel and to read widely in both art and literature. Throughout his life he took a deep pleasure in music, and politically he was a supporter of the Gladstonian Liberal party.

He went to Eton when he was 14 to the house of Henry Broadbent, a classical scholar whose teaching he respected, and he remained grateful to Eton for the pleasure he retained throughout his life in reading the classical writers. Owing to a weak heart he was unable to play any games, but he was more than content to be allowed to lead an individual and not a communal life, and he enjoyed having his own room, lit by candles, where he was expected to prepare his own breakfast and tea.

It was at Eton that he developed a strong admiration for Mr Gladstone and the Liberal Party and for the concept of liberty. He re-started the debating society in his house and developed a style of speaking carefully based on Mr Gladstone's own, whose speeches he used to read aloud to himself in his room. This style, with its excessive wordiness, caused great amusement to the other boys and he later reformed it; he was always willing, however, to amuse his children and their friends by taking some absurd topic and expanding on it in an exaggeratedly Gladstonian style of oratory.

Although Edward's father found plenty to enjoy at Eton, he regretted that his house-master took little interest in the boys and in the running of the house, where the discipline was very lax, and he was glad to leave at 18. He then went on to enjoy an intensely happy period at Balliol College, Oxford. There he made many lasting friends, some of whom later became public figures, and his room was always the focal point for gatherings because he had a piano in it; he could reproduce from memory any tune he had heard or improvise any style of music according to the mood required.

It was, however, the politics which particularly interested him at this stage and nearly all his friends were Liberals like himself. He became President of the Palmerston Club, though he did not speak at the Union as he judged his Gladstonian style to be unsuitable there. He was disappointed to leave Oxford with only a third-class degree, and in retrospect he feared that he gave too much time and energy to the excitements of political discussion. He then studied for the law examinations and was called to the Bar in 1902.

After the 1906 Election the House of Commons was full of his Liberal friends and he used to go there whenever he liked and be sure of a warm welcome. He was well-known to the Prime Minister, Sir Henry Campbell-Bannerman, for whom for a while he acted as an unpaid private secretary. In August 1906 he was staying with his parents in Marienbad when Lady Campbell-Bannerman died: his parents' sitting-room was next to her bedroom and through the communicating door there came the smell of chloroform. King Edward VII was also in Marienbad and at the funeral service he walked with the bereaved Prime Minister, followed by Edward's grandfather and Sir Squire Bancroft as the chief representatives from England. Later, in 1911, Edward's father's name was one of those on Mr Asquith's list of Liberal supporters whom he proposed to make peers to ensure the passage of the Parliament Bill.

In about 1905 Edward's father first joined the Balkan Committee, which was originally founded on a humanitarian rather than a political basis to help the Balkan Christians against the tyranny of Turkish oppression, especially in Macedonia. Later, he came to know James Bourchier, the distinguished *Times* correspondent, who believed that the prosperity of the Balkan peninsula could only be secured by the unity of the Balkans, and after he himself became chairman of the Balkan Committee in 1934 he was concerned with helping to further these aims.

During the First World War Edward's father was exempted from military service on account of his heart, but given military rank as acting British Commissioner for Serbia and sent to Corsica to administer the Serbian Relief Fund. After the war he ceased to practise as a barrister, but he kept his chambers in the Temple, where he went every day to meet his secretary and deal with his considerable flow of correspondence.

He travelled a great deal in the Balkans between the wars, and *The Times* noted in his obituary:

> He remained convinced that only in unity could the States of the Balkans find strength, that only by being strong could they avoid interference from outside, and that only by being generous, or if not generous at least just, to their racial minorities could they hope to enjoy the full benefit of internal peace, economical administration, and agricultural and industrial development. That his friendship was genuine and disinterested was widely recognised throughout the peninsula.[4]

He formed an especial friendship with the Bulgarian people and in 1938 he received an honorary doctorate from Sofia University; at the same time his portrait was painted by a Bulgarian artist to hang in the National Gallery in Sofia.[5]

Introduction

Edward's father was very much liked as a person: because he had no career to follow he had time to read a great deal – history, literature, politics, philosophy – and time to talk about what he had read. He frequently laughed, and disliked pomposity or rigid attitudes: he would ridicule those whom he thought self-important. He strongly urged religious tolerance and disliked High Church practices; as a young man he took an interest in Positivism and came to know Frederic Harrison, the disciple of Comte. His command of language was admired and he was considered an exceptionally good after-dinner speaker and letter-writer. He had a courteous manner and was tolerant and kind; he would give (but never lend) money to anyone who seemed to him to have a need, although his records show that he was constantly anxious about money, because the substantial legacy which he received from his father barely covered his expenditure. He gave 10 per cent of his income to charity as a matter of principle.

Children liked him because he made them laugh and he took a great deal of interest in his own children at all ages: enthusiastically playing the piano for musical bumps, or teaching them to play bezique or taking them to the National Gallery to see the early Italian paintings. He was always eager to discuss the books they were reading and ready to invite their opinions as though they were adults. At the end of his life he was deeply saddened by the war, saying: 'Civilisation has broken down in our time.' He felt that everything he had worked for had been destroyed and even his records in his chambers were burnt in a great fire-bomb raid on the Temple; he died a few weeks before the end of the war, aged 67.

To turn to the other side of Edward's family, he never knew his maternal grandparents for his mother, born in 1890, was orphaned at the age of 11. She and her sister were then given a home by her half-brother, John Grieg, who was 30 years older and in the Church; he later became Bishop of Gibraltar and the first Bishop of Guildford. She was Beatrice, daughter of Henry Grieg, and from her mother's family, the Mays, she inherited a strong musical strain. Her great-grandfather was Henry May, whom Grove calls 'an amateur musician and composer of considerable ability'; he was brother of Edward Collett May, who held a number of public appointments as a teacher of singing and an inspector of music. Edward Collett May's daughter was Florence May, the pianist and teacher, who was a pupil of Brahms and was also his biographer; she played many of Brahms's works in England for the first time, and she died in London in 1923.

The bishop and his wife did not succeed in making a happy home for his orphaned half-sisters, and Beatrice Grieg was glad to go to Dresden as a music student when she was 18, where she studied the cello with Professor Georg Wille. She was thought good enough to have been a professional cellist had she wished and it remained one of her greatest pleasures to practise and to play. At Queen's Gate before the war she had a teacher who came to the house, and she played chamber music with a quartet organised and led by a former fellow-student in Dresden.

Her other great interest, which Edward shared, was in gardening. She spent a great deal of time planning, and working in, the garden of the family home in Sussex, and Edward from childhood onwards used to discuss with her the choice of plants and shrubs. He later developed a special interest in bulbs and in roses, and would follow their breeding in order to find particularly attractive blooms and shades of colour which pleased him.

Edward's mother was a lively companion with an engaging and entertaining manner, though quite quick to take offence. She was elegant in appearance, with a great interest in clothes and an aptitude for choosing what was both becoming and fashionable. Before the war she greatly enjoyed a busy social life, but after the war she found it difficult to adapt to the changes that had taken place in society and to do so as a widow: increasingly she came to depend on Edward both for his company and for the direction of her life. Edward with great kindness did as much for her as he could, such as giving her tickets for the debates in the House of Commons or including her in his dinner parties of political friends; in any case, he enjoyed her company and her lively interest in his affairs, except when she expected more to be done for her than he could reasonably include in his busy programme. For the last few years of her life she became increasingly irrational with an illness which seemed to be hereditary, for her sister, who became a Carmelite nun, developed the same symptoms at the same age, and Edward had some hard problems to solve. He managed all the same to continue to oversee his mother's life as well as organise his own.

Edward's parents had been married in 1920 and he was born three years later. An elderly nanny was engaged to look after him and in 1926, when his sister Ann was born, a nursery-maid was added; in 1930 his brother Richard was born. Edward was a high-spirited and engaging child who, by his bright and affectionate nature, gave great pleasure to his parents and grandmother. 'With all his intelligence,' wrote his father on a faultless Latin translation paper completed when Edward was 7, 'we find him a good and loving little boy.' He is affectionately remembered as 'mischievous' by his nursery-maid, and he was evidently inventive in finding ways to upset the nursery routine and cause an outcry, which he enjoyed.

Edward taught himself to read by memorising the words of the hymns which his parents sang with him each evening at bedtime. His memory was good and he enjoyed following the memorised words in his own hymn-book while he sang. No-one specially encouraged him to learn to read but it was apparent that before the age of four he could do so. He learned numbers by reading them on the pillars of the houses in Queen's Gate as he was wheeled past in his pram. He used to ask his nanny to push him up to Kensington Gardens on one side of the road and to make the return journey on the other side where the numbers were higher and came in descending order. His mother did not think Edward particularly remarkable: as he was her first child, she supposed that whatever he did was normal for his age.

His religious education was undertaken by his grandmother, who was a devout believer of the Low Church. She used to hold a 'service' by her bedside every Sunday morning for her grandchildren and combined spiritual teaching with general instruction in manners and morals. Part of Edward's task at the service was to read aloud the text of the Creed and the Ten Commandments, while his baby brother was warned to sit still and remain silent, though given a barley-sugar sweet to help him do so. The grandmother had a pretty voice and led the singing of the hymns; these were often selected for their good choruses, so that no child was too young to join in by clapping the hands correctly in time with the music while singing, for example, 'O! That Will Be Joyful! When We Meet To Part No More'. When a hymn had no chorus she would often add one, by raising her hands after the last line of the verse and clapping to the repeated line, adding sometimes a small embellishment which the children quickly learned.

Edward enjoyed the Bible stories she read to him and when he was two she bought him both volumes of 'Line upon Line', little books published by the Religious Tract Society with simple arrangements of the Old Testament stories, of which he had a good memory for the names and plots.

Edward was to go to school at Wagner's, nearby in Queen's Gate, where the scholarly Orlando Wagner did not care to take boys until they could read and write at about the age of seven. Because Edward had already made so much progress on his own and was eager to learn more, he was sent at five and a half to a pre-preparatory school where he was the youngest child. His first end-of-term report illustrated the combination of ability and diligence which was to remain characteristic of him: in Arithmetic, for instance, his report was 'Excellent, takes great pains'; under 'deportment' the headmistress wrote: 'a most amusing and original child'.

Edward moved on to Wagner's school in September 1929 when he was just six, and about six months younger than the average age of the other boys in Form 1. At Wagner's the boys were well taught and worked hard: every week Edward brought home a small report tucked into the top of his sock which listed his week's marks in English, French, Latin and Arithmetic, and his consequent place in the form order. His last end-of-term report gave him first place in the top form and Mr Wagner wrote: 'He has exceptional ability and if he has good health, I shall expect great things of him.'

Edward's brother Richard was expected to follow him to Wagner's, but after going there briefly he proved to have learning difficulties which would now probably be ascribed to dyslexia but which in those days mystified his teachers. He therefore did not follow in Edward's footsteps at all, but had a governess until the war and later went to Millfield school. He was exceptionally good-looking as a child and loved by all for his charming disposition; he was something of a favourite with his mother, which she admitted when accused of this by Edward and Ann, though they accepted her explanation that Richard had difficulties at school which made life harder for him. Edward and his brother remained always on the best of terms and shared the interests of music and gardening. Their sister Ann was sent to morning school at the age of six, in the same month that Edward first went away to boarding school.

SCHOOL, THE WAR AND UNIVERSITY, 1933–50

In May 1933, at the age of nine, Edward went as a boarder to Abinger Hill school in Surrey: Michael Howard describes its situation and gives a picture of Edward's life there. This was not the preparatory school for which Edward had long been entered, but a last-minute change of plan. Edward's parents worried about the need to send him to boarding school at all at this age, and his father in particular feared to condemn him to the same kind of inhuman treatment which he remembered. He himself had not gone to boarding school until the age of 13, his last year before Eton, but he still felt uneasy when he thought of it:

> 'The Headmaster was a man of, no doubt, high character,' he wrote, 'but there was something sadistic about him which was rather repellent. I remember the early school before breakfast on winter mornings when, after having a cold bath, he used to take us in algebra. We were placed in a semi-circle round the blackboard and any boy who gave a wrong answer was rewarded with a smack on the hand with a cane. I remember our terror lest he should pitch upon us and I remember a boy falling down in a dead faint from fear.'[6]

He admitted that he himself never received any real ill-treatment, but he disapproved, too, of the desire in such schools to stamp out individualism in a boy:

> There was a tendency in the late 19th century to turn all children out in one mould, to force them to have the same interests and to adopt the same point of view. This was undoubtedly carried too far.

When news of Abinger Hill spread among their friends, therefore, it seemed to Edward's parents to be an almost perfect solution to the problem. It still prepared boys for the Common Entrance examination for Eton, but it was a school which had only been in existence for six years and was run by a young headmaster with a modern outlook. There were no rigid school customs based on traditions of the past, no desire to fit each boy into the same preconceived mould and no demand for unquestioning acceptance of religious practices. There were wide parklands in which the boys were free to wander and a proclaimed desire to provide a libertarian atmosphere.

On the scholastic side there were no 'forms' as in conventional schools, but following the Dalton plan the boys were placed in subject 'sets' according to their ability. Some periods of the day were left vacant for a boy to choose what he studied during that time, under the guidance of a tutor. A sympathetic music mistress encouraged Edward's interest in harmony and composition, and he received consistently high grades for his hard work and good progress in piano playing. In Edward's own view, he was made to work hard at the school; however, the Headmaster disliked the idea of 'cramming' boys, so it was agreed that Edward should not take the scholarship examination for entrance to Eton, for which a more conventional Headmaster would no doubt have wished to enter him. As it was, Edward passed into Remove at Eton, the highest place obtainable for the normal entrant, and high enough to absolve him from the need to 'fag' for a senior boy in his house.

For Edward, Abinger Hill seems to have been a success and he retained an interest in the comparative merits of 'setting' by subject rather than 'streaming' by form, which he later came to reconsider when he was studying the needs of the comprehensive school.

In the autumn of 1936 Edward went to Eton, to C. R. N. Routh's house, where he stayed for six years; he had a distinguished career as an Etonian and greatly enjoyed the life there. Looking back many years later at the teaching in his time, he noted that

> the domination of the traditional curriculum was almost as strong as ever, and the time-table still appeared to be based on the fiction that we were all potential classical scholars.

He doubted whether some boys were receiving an education best suited to their 'age, ability and aptitude' (quoting the 1944 Education Act) but he went on to say:

> The strengths of the system, to those of us who could cope, were very real. In the first place our teachers showed a real concern for the individual. In addition to our housemaster and a succession of form-masters, we each had a classical tutor who presided over pupil-room and watched over our progress: . . . my recollection is of teachers who expected high standards, and punished slovenly work, yet who were just as ready to praise.[7]

In September 1939 at the start of the Second World War Edward and his family were at Ockham, their house in East Sussex, as was usual during the school holidays. It was decided to leave London for the duration of the war, so the Queen's Gate houses were largely emptied of furniture and No. 63 was lent as a hostel for Yugoslav seamen. Several members of the household staff were called up almost at once, but other residents arrived. Edward's grandmother and aunt came from London, with their dogs, their maids and even two hospital nurses since the grandmother was poorly and bedridden. Edward's parents were both too old to be required to do war service, but his mother was appointed billeting officer for the neighbourhood, and Ockham itself received secondary school teachers and pupils from south London as evacuees; in the event, they did not stay for long but friendly relations were established, and several of the teachers and girls kept in touch with Edward's parents for some years.

There must have been about 35 people living at Ockham at this time, and much coming and going, but none of it greatly affected Edward; he was displeased, however, when his parents decreed that the plan to watch the Sussex v. Yorkshire cricket match at Hove must be cancelled owing to the preparations for war. It had become the favourite family treat in the summer to follow the Sussex cricket team when it spent a week each at Hastings, Eastbourne and Hove.

Ockham was 12 miles from the south coast, and after the fall of France the area was considered to be vulnerable to invasion: in 1940 the house was requisitioned by the Army and filled with troops. Edward remained at Eton, but his sister's London school moved to Dorset and his brother's to Devonshire, so his parents decided to look for a temporary wartime home within reach of those schools. Eventually they settled in a small manor house in Dorset, with a full complement of elderly household staff, mostly old friends from earlier days who asked to be given a home for the duration of the war.

In the autumn of 1939 Edward passed the School Certificate examination with eight credits, and moved then into the Sixth Form, where he specialised in history. A year later, in December 1940, he gained an open history scholarship to Christ Church, Oxford and the question arose as to when he should take this up, as he would become liable for military service at the age of 18. At first it was agreed that he should go to Oxford for one year when he was 17 and complete the course after the war, but eventually it was decided not to break up his Oxford career in this way but to postpone it completely until after the war.

In his last year at Eton, Edward turned from history to classics as his main subject:

'It is not that he has lost his interest in history,' his housemaster wrote to Edward's father, 'but five schooltimes of a subject after you have won your scholarship is a long time to fill in . . . It is highly satisfactory that he should take farewell of his History by coming out top of the Historians in Trials . . . There is no doubt that Edward is enjoying himself to the full. He runs the school, or a very large part of it and his time is well taken up with work which he does very well and which has got to be done by somebody.'

He went on to explain his reasons for not appointing Edward as Captain of the House:

Edward is not an ordinary boy: he is a law to himself and all his many successes have been due to the fact that Eton has recognised this and allowed him to go his own way. He could never beat a boy, and he cannot be unkind enough to substitute effectively his tongue for the cane.

Edward's parents thought this a wrong decision, and that it would have been good for him to have to perform the duties of house captain rather than be regarded as a special case, but Edward urged them not to dispute it with his housemaster.

He was by now in the house 'library', which meant that he had certain administrative responsibilities in the house but privileges, too, one of which was to be allotted junior boys to 'fag' for him. One of them[8] remembers that

It was the custom for a fag-master to tip his fag at the end of the half for services rendered: the rate for the job was about five shillings. Edward, however, had a much better system. Fagging for him entailed very little work as he never made unreasonable demands and in return I was free to ask him for help with my extra work; this help was invariably given with great good will. The result for me was that Eton became a happier place.

Edward was never a figure of fun to us Lower boys, although he might well have been owing to his unusually unathletic build and individualistic outlook on life. We all admired him enormously, and when he was awarded his cricket colours for scoring and made 9th man in Monarch for rowing we were all amused and delighted.

During his last four halves, from May 1941–July 1942, Edward was co-editor of the Eton College *Chronicle*. This was a four-page paper recording school events, published during term-time, for which the two editors took it in turns to write a leading article on a subject of their own choice. In his last half, Edward was secretary of the College Musical Society and throughout his time at Eton he greatly enjoyed the musical life there and his friendship with Henry Ley, organist and precentor of the College Chapel. When Edward left he presented a cup to the music school to be awarded annually to a string player. In his last half, too, he was Captain of the Oppidans, and at the end of it he won the General Paper prize, which his housemaster called 'probably the best test there is of a boy's knowledge combined with intelligence'.[9]

It had already been arranged through the headmaster that Edward, now due for war service, should be employed at Bedford on a secret assignment in the Foreign Office. It was judged that he had certain intellectual characteristics particularly required by the unit which had visited Eton and recruited him, and that he could be of considerably greater service in this way than if he were to join the Forces. None of his family had any idea of the sort of work he would be doing, but he came home for two days at the end of the half before going to Bedford to start a training course.

On arrival in Bedford, by a strange but happy chance, he was sent to the wrong billet where he was accepted without question because the household was expecting another man. In this way he found himself in the home of three very old people, the surviving children of the Rev. J. B. Dykes. Edward had long had a particular interest in the music of this Victorian writer of hymn tunes and was delighted to find himself lodging with his son, John Dykes, and his two octogenarian widowed sisters.

Not long after his arrival in Bedford, in October 1942, Edward was unexpectedly called up to the General Services Corps Training Wing at Norwich for military training as a private. He had not been a member of the OTC at Eton (his housemaster had advised against it) and he found the army drill and bayonet practice difficult to execute. He did his best to conform to the life and work in the camp but he was aware of his relative incompetence in dealing with the demands made of him.

His father, who was worried about the sudden change in his circumstances, managed to make the wartime journey to Norwich and Edward wrote to him the next day:

Ever since I left you last night I have been filled with remorse that I never said how pleased I was to see you – after you had taken the trouble to come all that way. In fact I rather gave the impression that I didn't want to be bothered with you at all! That was quite untrue: but as you can realise, I don't want to get into *unnecessary* difficulties with my sergeant, and it was just as well I got my clothes marked last night. We had a lecture this morning on shirking barrack duties . . .

He goes on to say that his training officer at Bedford is appealing against his transfer, and that he feels his father is unnecessarily pessimistic about his chances of returning there.

To this letter Edward's father appended a note:

He was not really inconsiderate, but it was a strain on both of us. I had travelled for 10 hours to have 1 hour with him, and he wanted to tell me everything. Within a week he was released to return to his old work, I am thankful to say.

And so it was. After 18 days at Norwich the sergeant told him: 'We've nothing for you here, Eddie,' and he was returned to Bedford with an Army report which read: 'Intelligent, but not a smart soldier either in appearance or on parade. Tries hard, but cannot adapt himself to army life.'

On his return to Bedford, Edward started a new course, and in his billet he found Mr Dykes and one sister laid up with bronchitis, so he had his meals alone with the remaining widow, aged 87, and took the opportunity to go through the family collection of J. B. Dykes's hymn tunes on the piano. 'They vary from alpha-plus to gamma,' he decided, 'but I enjoy them all. I think Ancient and Modern got the best of them. Many are very alike – certain harmonic tricks recur again and again.'

Edward's parents felt that he led a rather lonely life at Bedford, billeted with old people and unable even to talk about his work, but he wrote cheerfully to his father in November 1942:

Well, I have been back nearly a fortnight, and Norwich is already little more than a memory . . . The new course is great fun . . . The work is not harder, and I have as many friends as I want! I have plenty to read in the evenings, and the weeks are passing by like days. The situation with regard to the future is still obscure – I may be drafted into a particular section which will involve my 'rejoining the colours' . . . Whatever happens, I hope my reading here in my spare time will prepare me for the University after the War. Incidentally I read last weekend Brailsford's Voltaire – a delightfully lucid book, written refreshingly from the left point of view. The chapter on V's history is one of the best expositions of the 18th century outlook I have read. I will pass it on to you when we meet . . .

And so the letter continues, over several more closely-written pages, covering a wide range of subjects: gossip from a weekend visit to Eton (including doubts as to whether his former housemaster really understands 'constructive Metaphysics and critical Ethics'); comments about Socialist economics and unrestricted *laissez-faire*; a brief passage commending the 'neat composition' of the Saint-Saens cello concerto; and praise for the glories of Ely cathedral, which he places above Canterbury and Norwich but below Salisbury and Wells.

At the end of 1942 Edward left his training course and started to work at Bletchley Park, though he never spoke of what went on there until over 30 years later when the story of Bletchley was officially disclosed. Even then he never described his own part in the work. At the time, his father tried his hardest to get Edward at least to indicate the nature of his work, in order to satisfy the curiosity of Edward's grandmother who was nearly 90 but mentally very vigorous and lying bedridden in another part of Dorset. Edward was greatly displeased by this: surely he could see, he would complain to his father, that by making a request which he was legally bound to refuse he was putting Edward in an impossible position – but his father continued to press him.

Edward worked in a section which was predominantly military though he himself remained a civilian. He was interviewed with others at Bedford by the officer in charge of this section, who realised after a few minutes' talk that Edward had high intelligence and a remarkable memory; as he also had some knowledge of German he made him his first choice. Edward then became part of a team studying the communications passing between units of the German Army in medium-grade or low-grade cypher. The de-crypted material was passed to Bletchley from the intercept stations along the South Coast which later moved into Normandy with 21 Army Group. Edward's section was also responsible for ensuring that all intelligence from this source was made available to other sections at Bletchley to whom it might be helpful, and later to the American Army, which had its own organisation.

The German Army used the medium-grade and low-grade cyphers (Playfair and three letter codes) for intercommunication between all units from division downwards. All traffic from division upwards used the top secret Enigma cypher and so did not come into Edward's sphere for research work, though he later had unofficial access to Hut 3 where Enigma was handled.

It was not until the Normandy campaign began that the intercepts handled by his section produced much intelligence of value for until then these German units were more or less static and the volume of traffic was small.

Once the invasion began and the war became mobile the volume of traffic and the intelligence gleaned from it increased considerably. Edward's qualities were exactly those required for the creation and maintenance of a Map Room and he and one other member of his Section were detailed to take on this assignment. As the war progressed the Map Room became a matter of interest and not inconsiderable importance to other departments at Bletchley. It was decided that Edward should give a lecture in the Map Room every day at 12 noon which was open to all departments, and it was at this time that he had unofficial access to Enigma intercepts. The Map Room then became an important feature of Bletchley life and many people came to listen to the lecture and to look at the battle maps. The colleague with whom Edward worked at this time remembers that 'Edward had a photographic memory which was a godsend in times of stress. My abiding recollection of him is of an extremely conscientious man going to endless trouble to "get it right".'[10]

Despite frequent illness in the Dykes household Edward was able to remain there for two years, but in October 1944 to his sorrow he was obliged to move to a boarding house elsewhere in Bedford. He rarely had leave owing to the nature of his work; he was unable, for example, to attend his grandmother's funeral in 1944 but he did come home for four days to spend his 21st birthday with the family in Dorset, and had brief leave again to attend his father's funeral in March 1945.

After his father's death Edward's family responsibilities were immediately very greatly increased. He was the executor of his father's will and he took over his father's responsibility as co-executor of his grandmother's will, for his father had not had time to complete the dispersal of his mother's estate before his own illness and death, and much remained incomplete and contested. From this time on, a constant flow of letters – from tax collectors, accountants, beneficiaries, solicitors – followed Edward relentlessly, first to Bedford and later to Oxford. Only six weeks after his father's death came the end of the war, when the Army returned Ockham to Edward's ownership and a correspondence started about war reparations. The household in Dorset was disbanded and the family returned to Ockham, moving at first into just a few bare rooms. The two houses in Queen's Gate had been damaged by a land mine and needed either to be repaired or sold. Countless documents had to be produced, and many of them could not be found; in some cases they had been destroyed in the fire at the Temple where Edward's father had kept his papers in a safe, and his father's secretary, who would have known the answers to some of the queries, had died during the war. Much was lost, contested or misunderstood and all the unresolved problems came ultimately to Edward, aged 21, for arbitration and decision.

In the autumn of 1945, now 22 years old, Edward was released from his war work to take up his history scholarship at Christ Church, Oxford, where his tutors were Steven Watson and Hugh Trevor-Roper. If Edward's life at Bedford had been quiet, working with men older than himself and reading alone in the evenings, he plunged at once into a very different life at Oxford, renewing his friendship with a number of old Etonians and actively pursuing a busy social and political life. In 1946 he wrote to his mother:

> The Conservative Association here is flourishing, very full meetings and lively study groups. Thorneycroft came back to drinks. What with everything else you may be quite surprised to know that I produced an essay of 13 pages this week.

It was at this time that Edward decided to be confirmed: at Eton in 1938 he had refused this, which was an unusual step for a boy to take but it had been accepted by the school and by his parents, religious tolerance being a concept ardently supported by his father. By the time he came to Oxford he had already changed his mind and it was Canon Mascall of Christ Church who prepared him for confirmation by the Bishop of Oxford. Edward also turned to the High Church, and at the end of his life he spoke of music as having been the factor which drew him at this period to the Anglo-Catholic faith:

'I put on the old recording of the first part of the Dream of Gerontius,' he wrote to his sister in 1981, 'I don't think I have ever found the music quite so beautiful – e.g. the solo oboe at "in that Manhood crucified", the scoring at "novissima hora est", and memories of Tommy Armstrong spurring on the Oxford choir with his own quite nice tenor voice at the words "Who hath been poured out on thee" immediately before that magnificent choral entry at "go in the name of angels and archangels". This is music that has always made a strong emotional appeal to me, and it is silly to pretend otherwise – in fact I think it was in considerable measure a sheer accident that we sang it in the Oxford Bach Choir during my first year that brought about my "Anglo-Catholic period" which friends of mine, looking back, may otherwise find somewhat puzzling to understand.'

Edward studied the High Church movement, and he used to act as a server at the high altar of the Cathedral. In the autumn of 1946 he joined a group undertaking a mission in Yorkshire. 'Think of me on Friday when I give my talk on the Sacraments,' he wrote, 'Wednesday (I think it is) I serve Father Dean at the 8.30 Mass!'

Sir Thomas Armstrong was organist at Christ Church Cathedral at that time, and remembers Edward's interest in music, and in church music especially:

He was one of those naturally qualified to appreciate the beauty of the Anglican liturgy and its best music, and he had definite views about it, particularly about the singing of the Psalms . . .

It is interesting that you should mention 'The Dream of Gerontius', because I remember him talking about it, and being rather shy about his strongly emotional response to a work that was being harshly criticised by some of his contemporaries. But his response to music was always emotional – more so than he cared to admit and more so than was usual in Oxford.[11]

In addition to his other activities while at Oxford, Edward used to travel to London quite often to go to dances or other parties; he enjoyed dancing, which he did gently but rhythmically, talking all the time.

In 1947 he went on the Union debating tour of the USA about which Tony Benn writes, and when he returned in the Spring he was elected President of the Union for the coming term with an unusually large majority, topping 300 votes, which gave him a majority of votes over the three other candidates combined. It was the outgoing President, Tony Benn himself, who had generously proposed him and it was unusual for a Socialist to propose a Conservative candidate.

Edward also returned from America with a stated liking for American girls, whom he found attractive and entertaining. He once assured a journalist that he got on well with women, though he never cared for earnest women with an inclination to lecture him. What he liked best was to be made to laugh, which he did very easily and very often.

In March 1948 Edward's political future began to take shape, for he received a letter from Conservative Central Office saying: 'I would very much like to send in your name for any reasonable vacant candidature which comes along before or after redistribution.' By the end of that year he had been selected as candidate for the Perry Barr division of Birmingham.

Evidently in the summer term Edward felt some anxiety about the state of his studies, because on 12 June his tutor, Steven Watson, replied to an 'early morning letter' as follows:

> I can see how difficult the term has been and I am not very worried about it, provided you do those things we should have done. If I have not already done so I will sometime complete the list of essays I would have set you and the books to go with them.

There was some discussion that year as to whether he should return again in 1949 to complete his degree and take his finals Schools in June, and in the end, following advice from his tutors, it was agreed that he should do so. In February 1949 Edward reported to his mother: 'All goes well in Perry Barr.' In March he was in Birmingham for a meeting of the city Unionist Association, and for three dinner parties at which he found the formalities rather absurd. He also met the member for Handsworth, Harold Roberts, whose seat he later took over, and who told him that the first political speech he ever made was a vote of thanks to Edward's grandfather. In April Edward returned to Perry Barr to go canvassing before the local government elections; at the end of the month he was called to Sussex to replace his father by taking the British Legion ceremonies at Salehurst. On 2 May, when he was proposing to devote himself to working for the examinations, he was distracted again by the need to go to Birmingham for an eve-of-poll meeting before the council elections. At last he returned to Oxford, writing: 'Now I have gone back to school for the last time,' and saying that he found it hard to change from being a parliamentary candidate and president of an Association to being a glorified schoolboy again. At the end of the month he wrote: 'Finals Schools start on Thursday at 9.30. I cannot pretend that I dread the prospect quite as much as I should . . . '

In the event he was awarded a third-class degree, to the surprise of his tutors, both of whom had thought he had the potential to get a first-class degree. With hindsight, Steven Watson wished he had taken the examinations a year earlier.

There were no recriminations at Edward's home: 'I call it rather *chic*', his mother replied spiritedly to a friend who tried to condole with her; but Edward himself found no excuses and felt it rather badly.

IN PARLIAMENT AND IN GOVERNMENT, 1950–64

In the post-war general election of 1945, Birmingham had returned 13 members of Parliament; in 1948 there was a redistribution of these divisions, and although 13 constituencies remained, some of them had new boundaries and in some cases there were new names. Several of these redistributed constituencies then looked for a member, and at the end of 1948 Edward was invited to appear before the selection committees of three of them: Ladywood, Perry Barr and Yardley. At Ladywood he was not selected, but shortly afterwards at Perry Barr the committee invited him for interview as the only candidate, and recommended his adoption.

The Yardley committee was to meet only a few days later, and the city Agent advised Edward to delay his reply to Perry Barr as Yardley offered a better chance for a Unionist candidate of getting into Parliament, but Edward accepted the Perry Barr nomination unreservedly.

The influence of the Chamberlain family remained strong in Birmingham and Mrs Neville Chamberlain was still an active participant in the political affairs of the city, and a much respected figure. The 13 Unionist candidates were co-ordinated as a group by the Birmingham Unionist Association: this powerful central body, working in Empire House in the city centre, had an active leader in its President, Geoffrey Lloyd, who exerted a strong paternal influence on the candidates.

Introduction

When Edward contested the seat at Perry Barr in the General Election of February 1950 he lost it to the Labour candidate, who had a majority of 8000 votes. Later that year, however, the sitting member for Handsworth, Harold Roberts, decided not to seek re-election owing to ill-health, and Edward was invited to replace him as prospective candidate. At the end of September Alderman Roberts died and a by-election was held in November, which Edward won with a majority of 8231 votes. He was aged 27 and the youngest member of Parliament, but only for a fortnight, for on 30 November Tony Benn was elected at a by-election at the age of 25.

Handsworth was not one of the new constituencies: it had existed since 1918 and in the 1948 redistribution its boundaries had been left virtually unchanged. It comprised three wards: Handsworth, Sandwell and Soho, each returning three Unionist members to the city Council. It was a most desirable constituency for an aspiring Tory politician, as Edward recognised, and he appreciated the opportunity to learn about the municipal life of a great city, and to meet constituents with successful commercial and industrial interests, all of which were matters quite new to him.

As far as support for the Unionist party was concerned, the constituency had a feeling of confidence and permanency: most officers of the Handsworth Unionist Association were councillors or aldermen, some of whom had been or were later to become Lord Mayor of the city; at the other end of the scale there were innumerable small but thriving local branches of the Association, including many women's groups and groups for young people.

The constituency at this time contained quite a wide cross-section of people and dwellings: in some parts there were large houses set in extensive grounds and inhabited by prosperous people with resident maids. There were terraced houses substantially built but requiring post-war repairs and modernisation, and there was also a certain amount of poorer housing, as a municipal report of November 1950 explained:

> There are no real slums, but patches of older, smaller homes which do not measure up to the accepted standards of today. There are only a few groups of municipal houses.

There were still one or two farms in Handsworth in 1950, and Handsworth Wood still covered a considerable area, although by 1950 the trees were beginning to be cut down to make way for building sites. Much of the area was leafy, and sufficiently far from the city centre to seem a most desirable residential neighbourhood.

Edward was fortunate to find a political agent already in Handsworth, Harry Shires, who served him with the greatest loyalty for his 20 years as Member of Parliament and served the Unionist Party for 30 years. Inevitably, though, it became a disappointing constituency for a Conservative agent because the party's substantial majority was reduced during Edward's time, and his successor lost the seat to Labour in 1974. In 1979, after a further redistribution of Birmingham seats, the parliamentary division of Handsworth was abolished.

When Edward first arrived, however, the prospects seemed rosy: in the 1951 election he again had a majority of over 8000 votes, and in 1955, after another redrawing of the boundaries, he received more than 10 000. By 1955, too, he had had some parliamentary experience and could write: 'The Ministry of Supply has kept me in close touch with the progress of trade and industry in Birmingham and I know that the city has recently been enjoying the greatest period of prosperity it has ever known.'[12]

Edward did not until much later have a home in his constituency: it was easy to reach by train from London and he stayed when necessary in a hotel. It was his intention to sell Ockham, which seemed too large to manage and too costly to run, as well as impossible to staff. In 1950 he and his mother looked for a much smaller house in the country where she might live, while he would take a flat in London. But they failed to find anything they liked, while at the same time it seemed impossible to find a buyer for Ockham – the house was too large and the drive too long to attract offers in the relatively austere post-war conditions of the time. Finally, with relief, the search was abandoned and Edward kept the house for another 20 years until he moved to Leeds. It was his home and his only base in a life constantly on the move; there he had his books, his gramophone records and his garden and he came increasingly to enjoy it and to love getting back there.

It was Edward's grandfather who bought the property in about 1898, when he was engaged on a case for the South Eastern railway and took a liking to the neighbourhood. It was originally an outlying farm of the Abbey of Salehurst, built in about 1600, but little of the original Jacobean structure remained. The house lay three-quarters of a mile from the road, with a magnificent view from the entrance gate over the Rother valley towards the hills behind Hastings; even from the house itself, which lay considerably lower, the view was still far-reaching and delightful.

Edward's grandparents altered and enlarged the house, and his parents enlarged it still further, making the north side 'really pretty frightful'[13] according to Edward, but the south front retained much of its original character and charm. The abbey church of Salehurst and the few remains of the Abbey lay 20 minutes' walk away, separated by the A21 main road to Hastings.

Instead of being sold, the house was revived and Edward and his mother set about restaffing it. Chief in importance to Edward's life was the return to the family of the butler, Denis, who had originally come to Edward's grandmother as a footman 20 years earlier; Denis remained a stable figure at Ockham as butler and housekeeper and it was he who made possible the entertaining which Edward and his mother so much enjoyed and which Edward continued after her death.

Edward took his seat in Parliament at the end of 1950 and was fond of telling the story of his first meeting with his party leader. Mr Churchill sent for him, but was in a rather bad mood when Edward arrived at his room; for some time he ignored him, but finally he scowled a little and said grudgingly (and Edward used to imitate the voice, as he always did when telling anecdotes about people): 'They *say* you're promising.' A few days later Mr Churchill saw Edward in the House and hurried over to him, beaming in the friendliest manner, perhaps remembering that his initial welcome had been unenthusiastic; this time he enquired warmly (and again Edward would put on the Churchill voice): 'Are you settling down?'
from the house itself, which lay considerably lower, the view was still far-reaching and delightful.

Edward did settle down and he made his maiden speech in the Budget debate in April 1951. After the Conservative victory in October 1951 he was appointed PPS to Nigel Birch, at that time Parliamentary Secretary at the Air Ministry. In December 1952 Edward asked to be relieved of his duties as he had been appointed to the select committee on delegated legislation. Just over a year later, in February 1954, Harold Macmillan, who was then Minister of Housing, invited Edward to act as his temporary PPS while his official one was away ill, and at the same time to join the standing committee on the Housing Bill. In April Edward was appointed as one of the eight official delegates to the Council of Europe at Strasbourg, and then in July 1954 he was appointed to the government, as parliamentary secretary at the Ministry of Supply, where Duncan Sandys was minister. At the age of 30, Edward was the youngest member of the government, and he remained pleased and proud that he had served in Mr Churchill's last government.

The *Birmingham Post*, noting that Edward had entered the House less than four years before, observed: 'It is not often that proven talent receives such swift recognition.'[14]

The appointment was noted with pleasure in Handsworth, and the party annual report added:

> In spite of his Ministerial duties and many speaking engagements throughout the length and breadth of the country, your Officers note with pride that the Member visits Handsworth on every possible opportunity and continues to give many private interviews besides attending a wide variety of non-political functions. Sir Edward has one of the finest records of any MP having missed only 12 Divisions in the 232 taken during 1954 and of these 12 occasions he was officially 'paired' eight times.

In April 1955 Edward was further promoted, to be Economic Secretary to the Treasury and in June he went to Paris to represent the Treasury at the Paris meeting of the Ministerial Council of the OEEC. He attended a Cabinet meeting as the youngest Conservative Minister to do so since Mr Churchill in 1906. In September he went with the Chancellor of the Exchequer to Istanbul for the meeting of the World Bank and International Monetary Fund. In October he went to India and Singapore for the government, and in December, with the Foreign Secretary and Minister of Defence to a meeting of the NATO Council in Paris. In the Handsworth annual report, Edward was recorded as having represented the division 'with considerable distinction' and his career was seen as 'a source of great pride and satisfaction to the Association'.

Edward was in demand as a speaker all over the country at this time, and as something of a 'rising star' he was interviewed for an article in the *Queen* magazine. This is the picture presented of him at the age of 32, when Economic Secretary at the Treasury:

> The first thing you notice about Sir Edward Boyle is a complete absence of pomposity or affectation either in his manner or his appearance, which is big and well-scrubbed-looking and untidy, and somehow creates the impression that if you went through

his pockets you would find tangled bits of string and loose toffees. What you notice next is his kindness and his air of authority. . . . [15]

In December 1955 Harold Macmillan became Chancellor of the Exchequer and Edward came to know him well at this time; the long debates on the Budget resolutions and the Finance Bill lasted from April until July and Edward played a considerable part in them. Again this year (1956) he went abroad for the government, notably to the Baghdad Pact Council in Tehran and he also accompanied the Chancellor to meetings of the International Monetary Fund and World Bank in Washington.

All the promise of a golden future for his career came suddenly to an end in November when Edward, after some days of increasing anxiety and unhappiness, felt himself unable to support the government's policy over the Suez crisis, and asked the Prime Minister to accept his resignation. Both John Grigg and David Lane discuss this resignation.

Edward went to Handsworth to justify his action, first to the Executive Committee and then at a general meeting of his constituents held at Empire House. The room was packed for this meeting, and the general feeling was that in an international crisis verging on war, the members of a government have a duty to support the Prime Minister in the national interest, no matter what their private reservations may be. A former constituent who was present remembers the occasion:

> Without any trading of insults, the comments were frank, to say the least. I felt that this was one occasion when Edward lost the argument: his defence of his stance was not as convincing as I would have expected, and I felt the rejection of his views by the meeting justified on the strength of the arguments. A final comment that I particularly recollect: 'Well, at least tonight we have heard that rarity, a completely honest politician.' This indeed was the general opinion; and in retrospect both sides emerged with honour.[16]

The feeling that he had 'let down' Sir Anthony Eden by resigning at a time of national danger was widely held by Conservatives and his action was seen as 'unpatriotic' by some. However, despite the upheaval in Edward's life that this resignation caused, he was not left idle in the House of Commons and was quite shortly afterwards appointed a member of the standing committee on the new Rent Bill.

Following Sir Anthony Eden's resignation in January 1957 the new Prime Minister, Harold Macmillan, invited Edward to join his government as parliamentary secretary at the Ministry of Education; this was an offer which, after some thought, he was glad to accept. Again he was criticised by some, this time for returning to the government, and he himself wrote:

> I never had the least doubt that I was right to resign last November, though I was naturally extremely sorry to leave the Treasury. It was more difficult to decide whether or not to accept Harold Macmillan's invitation to come back. I am not absolutely certain that this was the right decision, but I certainly enjoy the work . . . and it would have been extremely difficult to have refused to serve someone who had been so very kind to me for nearly a year when we were together at the Treasury.[17]

Here began Edward's long association with education which subsequently became his principal field of concern, whereas previously his chief interest had been in the economy. The Minister of Education appointed in January 1957 was Lord Hailsham so that Edward had the responsibility of speaking for the Ministry in the House of Commons, until in September 1957 Lord Hailsham was succeeded by Geoffrey Lloyd. In December 1957 the government published the White Paper *Secondary Education for All*, the largest single programme for developing the educational services since the 1944 Act, and Edward had particular responsibility for presenting the government's programme of extended technical and scientific education; he was also the principal government spokesman when the general grant orders were debated in the House of Commons.

Edward led the United Kingdom delegation at the UNESCO conference in Paris in November 1958, where he saw 'just how great is the need for all the overseas assistance which Britain can afford'. By October 1959 he could claim: 'During the past two and a half years I have visited just over half the 146 Local Education Authorities in England and Wales.'

'Visitors from abroad,' he said, 'regard our 4000 schools since 1951 as one of Britain's finest post-war achievements. I am sure they are right . . . The nation is indebted to the teaching profession – notably in the Primary schools – for the manner in which they have coped with larger numbers during the past ten years . . . The Conservatives are determined to see that children in all secondary schools are given opportunities and incentives to the full limit of their abilities.'[18]

He also promised more technical colleges, an increase in university students by at least one third and an expansion in teacher training colleges by nearly two thirds.

After the October 1959 general election (at which his majority remained at over 10 000 votes) Edward was re-appointed to the Treasury as Financial Secretary. Here he served under two Chancellors: first, Derick Heathcoat Amory, and from July 1960 Selwyn Lloyd. He was immensely happy at the Treasury and played a leading part in many of the debates in the House, not only in supporting the annual Finance Bill but also, for example, speaking on proposals for aid in two areas in which he had already become particularly interested: education, and aid for developing countries.

It was during these first years of Edward's career in Parliament that his domestic life was complicated by his responsibility for his mother. She died at the end of 1961, but for a few years previously she had been showing signs of instability in her behaviour. Little was clearly understood at the time, and it was only after her death and looking back that Edward was able to trace the course of her illness and see it as a gradual decline. He had to contend with many problems, including demands on his own time, but he was extraordinarily tolerant and patient. He did not allow himself to become harassed by the situation, though it was undoubtedly distracting, and his mother lived at home until she died.

Not long before her death he was best man at his brother Richard's wedding and arranged a reception at the House of Commons. He subsequently always kept in touch with his brother's family, visiting them regularly and having them to stay; he took trouble to provide appropriate treats for his three Boyle nephews and he was always responsive to requests for advice or practical help.

In July 1962 Edward was appointed to the Cabinet as Minister of Education, and this period, 1962 - 64, was perhaps the happiest of his life. Following his mother's death, he was able to give up his flat in Westminster with its temperamental Swiss housekeeper and for the rest of his life his 'home' in London was the Carlton Club, which he found convenient and peaceful. As a Cabinet minister he was allotted a car and a chauffeur which he found a great joy; he never tried to drive a car himself, and he had become accustomed to a life on the move when he was constantly hurrying from place to place carrying suitcases, briefcases and books. On excellent terms with his official driver, he enjoyed discussions about routes and points of interest on the journey, as well as the pleasure of switching on the car radio to hear the music on the Third Programme.

After the resignation of Mr Macmillan in 1963, Edward was a strong supporter of Mr Butler for the post of Prime Minister, but when Mr Butler himself agreed to serve in Lord Home's government Edward followed his lead.

Edward's most controversial act as Minister was to refuse to approve the pay scales for teachers' salaries agreed by the Burnham committee after negotiation between the two bodies affected: the teachers' union, the NUT, and the Association of Education Committees, representing the employers. In Edward's view, there needed to be some financial incentive for teachers to stay in the profession: too many young teachers were leaving after an expensive training and only brief service, and Edward believed that salary increases (for which the total sum had been agreed) should be weighted towards the higher end of the scale. The sums of money involved were relatively small – for a teacher on the lowest grade it was the difference between £650 a year on the proposed Burnham scale, and £630 as proposed by the Minister – but there was an important principle involved: it was the first time a Minister had sought to exert his authority in this way. The House of Commons debated the issue in April 1963 when Edward told the House: 'Teacher supply is the key to educational advance . . . the Burnham Committee provisional agreement seemed to have got the balance wrong. It gave too much weight to the young and inexperienced teacher and too little to the older.'

Edward took the unusual step of introducing the debate and winding it up too, because he knew he was inviting trouble and he preferred to handle it himself, feeling confident he was making the right move. A few weeks before, he had rung up his sister to say: 'There is going to be a row, but I'm sure I'm right.'

During the course of the debate he received strong criticism from the Opposition and heard himself condemned as a 'dictator'; some members of his own party abstained from voting, but the bill was passed with a majority of 50 votes.

In October 1963 Edward received the Robbins Report on higher education, and welcomed its recommendation for a greatly increased number of universities. He himself later selected what he felt were the two most important actions he took during his term of office as Minister. The first was the raising of the school-leaving age to 16. This was a recommendation of the Newsom Report which Edward received in October 1963. Edward firmly believed that the extra year would be valuable, allowing a four-year course of secondary education to be planned, and he announced that the proposal would be implemented in the year 1970/71. This news was received with a loud laugh in the House of Commons: it seemed to many members of the Opposition to be a date absurdly far ahead for an action said to be so earnestly desired by the Minister. However, despite the necessary delay, Edward was pleased and proud to have made the commitment.

The other matter to which Edward gave high importance was his action in effecting a single Department of Education and Science in April 1964, to cover all branches of education. This was against the recommendation of the Robbins Report which preferred to keep higher education separate, and to some extent against Edward's own interests, since the Minister of Science was Quintin Hogg, who was senior to Edward in the Cabinet. However, Edward was confident that a single department was by far the better choice and he fought for it with great determination, at the same time assuring the Prime Minister that the problem of two ministers equally eligible for one post need not be an impediment: he was perfectly willing to give way to Mr Hogg. In the event, Edward was appointed Minister of State with special responsibility for Science, and he was invited to retain his seat in the Cabinet on a personal basis.

IN OPPOSITION, 1964–70

In the 1964 General Election, Edward's majority in Handsworth fell from 10 000 in 1959 to just under 5000, and in the election of 1966 his majority was only 1200, making Handsworth a marginal seat. The constituency organisation was as active and as enthusiastic as ever, but the decline in the Conservative vote reflected both boundary changes and the changing nature of the area. From the 1950s onwards, as old-established families died or moved away from Handsworth, so new arrivals of Asian or Caribbean origin often moved in; they filled jobs in the city such as transport and nursing, as they did elsewhere in the country. They moved in at first to some of the larger properties coming to the end of their lives, where several families shared the same house and were willing to put up with shabby conditions and the lack of modern facilities. Where coloured families moved in, the area seemed to white residents to have become less desirable and those who could do so often moved away; those who stayed sometimes became the objects of commiseration or even of scorn, and friction resulted from the anxieties and irritations of the situation.

There was no mention of the issue in Edward's 1964 Election Address, but he did include it in 1966, calling it 'a matter of prime importance to Handsworth'. In 1968 the Labour Government brought in the Race Relations Bill: 'I am a bit critical of the Bill, but more because I think it needs strengthening than because I want to see it emasculated,' Edward wrote, and he abstained from voting for the Conservative amendment, as David Lane describes. Most Conservatives in Handsworth saw the Bill as being far too lenient over the question of limiting the rate of immigration: they would have preferred a 'quota' system. Edward was adamant in all his speeches in Handsworth that there should be 'no second-class citizens' and that 'Commonwealth subjects, who settle in this country permanently, should have proper rights and responsibilities of normal citizenship'. He had support on the platform from his divisional officers, but there was no doubt that in the constituency there was strong feeling about the issue, and those whose lives were most affected by it felt Edward to be too much concerned with the moral issues involved and insufficiently understanding of the practical ones. At the same time, it could be said that Edward's very concern for the moral aspects kept a potentially explosive situation at a lower temperature and forced a rational discussion of the matter.

Other Conservative-held seats in Birmingham felt the swing to Labour in the 1966 election, and in fact the 5 per cent swing in Handsworth was the lowest in the city, while only four Conservative members were returned for Birmingham city as a whole. Edward did not stand again, and although his successor held the seat in 1970 the new coloured population mainly supported the Labour Party, and with further boundary changes the seat was lost to Labour in 1974.

In Parliament Edward served on the Opposition front bench from 1964-69, briefly responsible for home affairs and then from February 1965 acting as chief spokesman for Education. He also served from 1965-68 as deputy chairman of the Conservative Party National Advisory Committee (of which Mr Heath was chairman) with special responsibility for policy groups. In 1968 at Mr Heath's request he visited all the university Conservative Associations and made many visits to colleges and other centres of education.

Being out of office Edward was able to take up new interests and he was much in demand. In the catalogue of his papers deposited at Leeds University there is a list of about two hundred societies and other activities in which he played some part, and many of these interests were first taken up during this period. A few of those which were more central to his life will be mentioned here.

Perhaps first in importance at this time was his connection with Penguin Books. It gave him particular pleasure when Sir Allen Lane, to his surprise, suggested to him that he might care to join the board of Penguin's, and take on a special responsibility for the school textbook series which was becoming an important feature of the Penguin list, as well as a new and innovatory series on education. Charles Clark was the editor of this series and came to know him well:

> Edward's influence, both professionally and personally, extended in the happiest way throughout Penguin Books, but his achievement was precisely that pervasive influence, a 'climate of opinion' to borrow from W. H. Auden, not a readily reckonable set of doings that marked off this or that year of his time with Penguin's.
>
> He cared deeply about *books*, not at the end of the day about authors, publishers, marketing, cash flow, return on capital employed, etc. (although he understood, of course, all these things). What mattered to Edward was the worth of the books we published and what they had to say to their readers – in that, he resembled quite strikingly Allen Lane himself.
>
> He had financial, professional and intellectual independence, and he drew on it with endless caring, generosity and insight to steer many of us through crises great and small in the final years of Allen's life. His perhaps greatest quality was a kind of democratic empathy. He could judge shrewdly what really mattered in an agenda strewn with value judgements as much as with facts, and he could also recognise that what might be small in strategy might loom very large in the working life of a member of staff.

Edward spent a good deal of time at the Penguin offices at Harmondsworth and in discussion with Sir Allen Lane, not only over current policy but also about the question of ensuring a satisfactory future for the company after Sir Allen's retirement or death. In 1966 Sir Allen wrote to propose that Edward be designated to succeed him as chairman after his retirement, but Edward did not wish to make such a move away from politics at this stage:

> 'I greatly appreciated your very kind letter to me concerning the chairmanship,' he wrote, 'and do let me make it clear that – from now on – whatever happens to me in politics, I look on my link with Penguins as something definite and *lasting*; in other words any help or advice I can give is at your disposal anytime. I do indeed feel tremendously attracted by your offer, and my only reasons for wavering are a) that an announcement that I was going to succeed you as chairman in 1969 would, I fear, be misunderstood – commentators would say I was obviously writing off the prospect of a Conservative win at the next election; and b) I know it would be regretted by my friends if I were now to write myself off, irrevocably, as a possible candidate for office in the 70s.

In 1967 he was for a short time managing director of Allen Lane the Penguin Press, when the new hardback publishing subsidiary was set up in London in Vigo Street.

Edward gave considerable thought to several schemes put forward to him for the future of Penguin, and during Sir Allen's illness in 1968 he chaired all the board meetings and was in constant touch with Sir Allen during his illness and convalescence. In 1969 he was appointed vice-chairman. In April 1969 he organised a large and splendid dinner party in the House of Commons to celebrate the golden jubilee of Sir Allen's first entry into publishing. After Sir Allen's death in July 1970, he was briefly acting chairman, and Kaye Webb[19] remembers:

> It was a difficult, uneasy sort of time; we were being required to make far-reaching decisions which would have a profound effect on our future buying and marketing plans. Yet Edward, usually arriving with only minutes to spare, and never having time to stay for lunch, brought with him a calm competence

which infected us all, so that after summarising the position to everyone's satisfaction rather like a good headmaster, he would then disappear back to London, clutching last-minute sandwiches which I made for him to eat in the car.

Edward was subsequently closely involved with the plans to arrange a merger with Pearson, Longman; he later served on the Pearson, Longman board and on the Pearson board.

During this period, Edward served on several government committees. From 1966-70, for example, he was a member of the Fulton Committee, set up to examine the structure, recruitment and management of the Civil Service; he was a regular attender of the meetings, to which Robert Neild refers as a fellow member.

In the case of the Pearson Commission on International Aid and Development, which met in Canada in 1968 under the chairmanship of Lester Pearson, Edward was appointed as the UK representative. He counted his service on this committee as one of the most influential experiences of his life, partly because of his long-standing interest in India and in the needs of the developing countries, and partly because of his admiration for the personality of the chairman:

> One felt that Mr Pearson, with his combination of reason and conviction, his genuine feeling for the poor and despairing, and his unwillingness to be 'bought cheap' by anyone, was the ideal world statesman to introduce a meaningful dialogue on the crucial theme of the growing gap between the rich and poor nations

he wrote in *The Times* after Lester Pearson's death. From 1964–72 Edward served as a member of the Council of the Institute of Race Relations, and he gave advice and support to many groups active in this field. In the House of Commons he defended his views on race relations against considerable opposition, as David Lane describes.

Edward was appointed to the Arts Council in January 1966 and served on the Council for three years. He also served as deputy-chairman of the music panel in the years 1967 and 1968, and for two further years as a member of the panel. In October 1968 he was appointed to chair a committee of enquiry investigating the range of new activities in the Arts currently being developed by young people, and to recommend what the Council's attitude should be towards activities for which the traditional methods of assessment might not apply. The recommendation was to set up an advisory committee, and Edward served on this New Activities advisory body, which reported at the end of 1969.

In music, he was invited by the *Spectator* in 1967 and 1968 to do occasional reviewing of opera in London, deputising for their regular music critic. At Glyndebourne Edward was appointed a trustee in 1965; he retired in 1975 when he could no longer give the time to travel to the meetings in Sussex, though he remained a member of the Council until his death. Glyndeborne was only half an hour's drive from Ockham and Edward's mother had attended the first season in 1934; after the war he joined her and then never missed a season until his death.

When he became a trustee he had the added pleasure of being entitled to use the Glyndebourne box once a year; this held ten people, and enabled him to invite people whom he felt might not otherwise get the opportunity to go to Glyndebourne, which he particularly liked to do. He used to look forward each year to the arrival of the forthcoming programme, and going to Glyndebourne was latterly the only form of holiday he took, for he was disinclined to go abroad simply for the purpose of a holiday, though he was eager to see the historical sights and the art galleries when he was abroad for some official reason.

He was a founder trustee of the Winston Churchill Memorial Trust, and he served on the Pilgrim Trust from 1968–81. He was a member of the award committee for the Harkness Fellowships from 1967–72 and took a particular interest in the selection of these Fellows, partly because of his admiration for America and his feeling for the importance of England's close relationship with the American people.

Almost the last of Edward's official duties as Minister in 1964 had been to entertain the Czech Minister of Education when he came to London, and he himself (with his sister) was invited to Czechoslovakia in return in September 1965, even though the government by then had changed and Edward was no longer in office. He had already established a friendly relationship with the Minister – who had commended the 'very nice atmosphere' of the dinner party which Edward gave for him in London – and Edward greatly appreciated the return hospitality for ten days, which enabled him to see much of Prague, the University at Brno and more briefly the city of Bratislava. It was the kind of trip Edward enjoyed, involving long and hard-working days of visits and speech-making with concert-going in the evening, and throughout it all, either directly or through an interpreter, lengthy discussions with his hosts about education, European history and Marxist philosophy.

In 1965, too, Edward was invited to Leeds University to receive an honorary degree, one of eleven which he received over the years. At the ceremony he made a thoughtful speech of thanks on behalf of the honorary graduates, reflecting on the nature and value of the great civic universities such as Leeds and their contribution to the spread of knowledge. Several people asked for a copy of the speech afterwards, but he had nothing to give them as it was his custom only to write down headings on a card.

A few years later the university was looking for a new Vice-Chancellor to take office in October 1970, and William Walsh takes up the story of the approach to Edward. The proposal appealed to Edward, for he admired the university and its distinguished former vice-chancellors, and he liked the idea of having a full-time professional job. As far as the House of Commons was concerned, he felt that he had been spokesman for education long enough, and that there was only one office which particularly attracted him, that of Leader of the House; however, he judged that he was not senior enough to be offered the position in the next Conservative administration. He decided to write for advice to Lord Butler and evidently he was not discouraged by Lord Butler's reply. Edward always maintained that he left politics because he wanted to accept the opportunity offered at Leeds: 'It was the pull of the job I was offered and not, in any sense, a push away from politics that influenced me here,' he said in 1970. At the same time, he judged that his 'style' was probably not appropriate for high political office in the 1970s; some members of the parliamentary Conservative party treated him coolly as being undesirably 'left wing', while members of his own front bench made no serious effort to dissuade him from accepting the offer at Leeds. It was a decision which he made without great difficulty and one which he never regretted, so that in 1972 he could say publicly: 'I enjoyed the House of Commons very much, but I enjoy this much more.'[20]

Edward retired as spokesman for education in October 1969, when his place was taken by Mrs Thatcher, and at the dissolution of Parliament in May 1970 he retired as Member for Handsworth, where the people, the places and the problems had become a part of his life, and he remained in touch with the area. Looking back nearly 20 years later, a former constituent and Conservative supporter wrote:

All people in public life have their fans and their critics. Edward's admirers greatly outnumbered his critics – not only in Handsworth but in Birmingham as a whole and his retirement left a gap which hasn't been filled.[21]

Edward was determined to prove his commitment to the University of Leeds by selling Ockham and moving there permanently. He did not wish to be a southerner, temporarily working in the north, but rather to transfer his life to Yorkshire and learn to think and feel as a northerner. Although the job was the deciding factor in the decision to sell his home he knew that in any case he needed to make such a move soon; not only was Ockham costing him more than he could afford, but by 1970 most of his elderly staff wished to retire and were impossible to replace. He had become devoted to the place, and especially to the garden, so that after he left he used to return each year for an hour to two to see how the trees and shrubs had done.

When the house was put on the market the most likely purchaser only wanted it if the house were left fully furnished and equipped. In fact, this suited Edward very well, for he was seriously short of time and such a plan simplified the arrangements he needed to make. He had other furniture elsewhere: in his flat in Handsworth, for example, and in store from his flat in Westminster, so from Ockham he needed only to take such family possessions as he wanted to keep. He left the house in October 1970, after gathering together his little group of household and garden staff – three of whom had first worked for his grandmother – to sign the visitors' book with him on the final page. Then he left for London and gave dinner to his sister and her family, reminding them that now he owned no home nor any piece of land except the family burial plot in Salehurst churchyard. This later became a fact of more significance than he might have expected at the time, for with the high inflation of the 1970s and the subsequent rise in property value from which he could not benefit he was financially in a poor position. At the time he sold Ockham, house prices were low and the whole property fetched a very modest sum. Edward was extraordinarily generous – to his brother especially, as he had been also to his mother, and in smaller sums to everyone all the time – so that such generosity encouraged people to think of him as a rich man. In fact, he regularly spent more than he could afford, though little on himself, and when later he became ill and realised that the nature of the illness was likely to prevent him from working and earning a salary, this added a further anxiety but one of which he hardly ever spoke.

AT LEEDS UNIVERSITY, 1970–81

The Vice-Chancellor's Lodge at Leeds was a small, rather severe-looking mid-Victorian house with later additions, the most recent being a large music room made for the previous Vice-Chancellor, Sir Roger Stevens. The only additions for which Edward asked were book-shelves, so that he might take all his books and all his gramophone records from Ockham. The house was set in a large, flat garden and darkened in summer by well-grown trees standing close to it. Its position at the head of a short, steep road and cul-de-sac made it peaceful and secluded even though it was only two miles from the city centre. A gate in the wall of the garden gave access to the well-wooded ridge of Meanwood valley where winding paths between shrubs provided a pleasant walk to Headingley, much shorter than the journey by road.

Edward liked the house and garden immediately, and he quickly made it seem as though it had long been his own home. The Lodge was partly furnished by the University, but the sitting-room was empty and into it Edward put familiar furniture and ornaments: on the shelves beside the fire-place, for instance, he set out his grandmother's collection of Russian and Bulgarian icons, which had been in the dining-room at Ockham. The large music room was already furnished, but Edward added his father's Bechstein piano and his own record player, and hung on the walls the Piranesi prints which had been in John Morley's study and bought after his death by Edward's father, a great admirer of the Liberal statesman. As for the garden, Edward planned the planting of it with the same enthusiasm as at Ockham; he introduced bulbs, roses and flowering shrubs, ordering new stock himself from the numerous catalogues which came to him. In the Sunday evening telephone calls to which Georgina Dunlop refers, it was invariably the news of the garden which took first place as it had been from Ockham. 'Well,' he would start, 'the daffodils are all out now and Moon Goddess is looking, if anything, even lovelier than last year.' No matter how late in the day he returned to the Lodge, if it were still light enough he would go round the garden and offer to take others too. His University chauffeur remembered eager invitations to come and see the roses at the end of a long and tiring day.

When Edward moved to Leeds he had far fewer domestic responsibilities than he had ever had before and he enjoyed the relief this brought him. The maintenance of the Lodge was undertaken by the University, which had a building and works department ready to deal with problems and effect repairs. He used to say, too, that he had never before been so well looked after both at home, where the housekeeper who came to the Lodge in the mornings arranged his household affairs quietly and efficiently, and in his various public and private activities. He had had part-time secretarial help in the House of Commons, and had managed to cope with the many additional sides of his life by carrying a great deal in his head, by not worrying about a certain amount of confusion and by telephoning rather than writing a letter when pressed to deal with a matter. When he came to Leeds he had the full-time support of a Vice-Chancellor's office run by an experienced secretary who also acted as his personal secretary; he noticed the easing of the burden he had been carrying for most of his life and was correspondingly grateful.

From time to time in the first years at Leeds, Edward's butler Denis, now retired, used to come for a few weeks for special occasions, such as a visit by the Chancellor; when he was there, the Lodge seemed even more like Edward's 'home'. He was aware all the same that the Lodge was University property and that while living there he had a responsibility to entertain the University's guests; this he was happy to do and he felt that there was no conflict between the private and the public uses of the Lodge, but that University visitors would find it more interesting to come to his home rather than to a University department. He particularly enjoyed giving small dinner parties at the Lodge, to mark the retirement of a professor, for example; alternatively, after a large dinner party in the University he liked to invite a small group of people back to the Lodge afterwards for drinks and further conversation.

Edward was enthusiastic about the fine scenery and buildings of Yorkshire, and he liked to organise occasional sightseeing trips into the Yorkshire Dales, or a tour of abbeys and cathedrals. After his University chauffeur retired in 1975 he firmly refused to be provided with a new car and driver: while cuts were being imposed on University expenditure he thought it right that the Vice-Chancellor should absorb a certain share of them, and despite strong opposition from the University he maintained his view that a car was a luxury which he could well do without by walking to his office. And so he did, setting off in good time each morning for the downhill walk of about a mile, and using the bus to come home.

In connection with his position in the University, Edward attended meetings of the Committee of Vice-Chancellors and Principals (CVCP). He was the first politician to become a Vice-Chancellor and when he first attended the committee he was conscious of his non-academic background and spoke rarely, though he was listened to with respect when he did so. It was noticed that although he was not an academic by profession his principal concerns were those of an academic: that is to say, the welfare of students and of staff and the quality of the teaching and research came first with him, and political and financial aspects came second. His particular contribution to the committee was his knowledge of how government works and his familiarity with the ways of Whitehall and Westminster, as well as his personal contacts with politicians and civil servants.

In the two years 1977–79 Edward served as chairman of the CVCP, and in this position he was in his element. To some extent he was re-entering a world with which he was already familiar, absorbing government directives and negotiating their terms; his familiarity with government machinery and his sense of the political climate enabled him to perform a valuable role for the Committee at this time. He is remembered as:

> a superb Chairman, masterly in introducing agenda items, in encouraging and listening to discussion, and in summarising the tenor of the debate and reaching conclusions. He was receptive to a well argued case from whomsoever Vice-Chancellor it came, alive to the political realities of his day and not a little apprehensive about what would happen when the Conservatives came to power in 1979 in the light of their commitment to cut public expenditure as it had never been cut before.[22]

Edward continued to attend meetings of the CVCP during his illness, which came immediately after his retirement as Chairman at a time of great stress for universities, defending the welfare of his own institution almost to the end of his life.

When Edward resigned from the House of Commons, it was a great pleasure to him to be offered a life peerage on the recommendation of the Prime Minister, Harold Wilson, in June 1970, so that he still had a place in the Houses of Parliament. He took his seat in

June 1971 when he gave a large and happy lunch party in the House of Lords, entertaining not only his two supporters, Lord Butler and Lord Fulton and their wives, but also members of his family and close friends. In the House of Lords, where he sat on the cross benches, he found many former colleagues and friends and many debates in which he would have been glad to take part, so that he regretted that his duties restricted him to infrequent attendance at the House. He felt that his membership of the House of Lords would enable him to retain some contact with the political world he had left: in fact, he found himself less cut off from this world than he had anticipated. Former parliamentary colleagues kept in touch with him by letter or telephone to Leeds, and when he came to London for meetings he frequently spent the evening with friends from Westminster or Whitehall who had expressed a wish to see him in order to discuss some current issue with him. Although by his move to Leeds Edward seemed to abandon politics, in fact he was to some extent still retained within the political sphere.

Edward's wide range of contacts was an asset for the University: quite often, for example, he would be approached by a member of staff or by a student to suggest a suitable speaker for a special occasion – to celebrate, perhaps, the centenary of a notable figure or event – and his up-to-date knowledge of leading figures in various fields enabled him to make valuable suggestions.

He remained in demand all over the country as a speaker and he spent a great deal of time preparing his speeches and lectures. In many cases, though, there was no full script as he spoke only from notes based on his own reading and on the research done for him by his personal assistant. In the University, too, he spoke frequently and he had a special connection with the School of Education, where he played a small part in the teaching programme, lecturing on British educational policy during the previous 20 years and conducting occasional seminars.

Many of his outside speaking engagements were on the subject of education and he continued to develop his own ideas in the light of past experience and current trends. While both main political parties became increasingly polarised in their attitudes, Edward remained on middle ground somewhat distant from both. It was not that he considered education to be a non-partisan issue: 'Conservatives,' he wrote in 1976, 'were just as committed to the ideal of secondary education for all. But they believed that there must be priorities, and that over-ambitious plans which outstripped resources would only jeopardise those benefits of the 1944 Act which it was most essential to preserve.'[23] He continued to wrestle with the problems of correctly identifying the priorities both in the provision and the allocation of resources.

Edward was certain that selection at ten years old, and the consequent segregation of children living in the same neighbourhood as soon as they moved from primary to secondary school, was wrong. He studied the different needs of different areas in the country, and came to feel that comprehensive schools to the age of 16, followed by sixth form colleges, might be an acceptable solution in many areas. He was also interested in the value of middle schools, from ages 9–13. In large city areas he felt that there was often a special need for a direct-grant grammar school to act as a 'safety net' for specially able children whose parents were not well-off, and he did not wish to see such schools encouraged to move out of the public sector altogether.

As far as higher education was concerned, he regarded the setting up of a funding agency for the polytechnics and colleges to be a mistake: these institutions remained the responsibility of the local authorities and were best supported by them. In the case of the universities, he greatly regretted the reduction in financial support and increase in government control of spending which had already made a considerable impact on the universities by the time he died. He was worried that so many of his parliamentary colleagues were relatively ignorant about the universities: about what they stood for and what they did. After a year or two at Leeds, Edward determined to remedy this by inviting Members of Parliament to stay with him for a night and spend the following day in the University. His scheme, however, was not a success: sometimes MPs would accept the invitation to stay and would meet a few people at the Lodge, but they were always too busy the next day to spend time in the University as he intended, to learn about the work and visit the departments. He himself was active to the last weeks of his life in representing the interests of the Universities and in trying to secure from the government a better understanding of the nature of their contribution to public life, especially the large civic universities such as Leeds which he called the 'workhorses' of the system.

As well as writing speeches and lectures, Edward wrote a number of book reviews and articles for newspapers and other periodicals. These usually, though not always, were on educational or political topics, or in connection with his musical interests. Philosophy was another of his major interests, and of living philosophers he had a specially high regard for Karl Popper, about whom he wrote several articles. In 1971 he wrote:

> Popper is a great and humane thinker, who has devoted his intellectual life to a rigorous examination of the conditions of scientific and social progress. He is in the great tradition of those thinkers, and those writers, who are not utopians nor pessimists, but *meliorists* – spurred on not by the love of fame but the determination to do their best with whatever is to hand . . . '[24]

The concept of meliorism and the idea that the world is capable of improvement was one which appealed to Edward, and one which often guided him in his choice of action.

Christine Challis speaks of the value to Edward of the overnight train service from Leeds to London, which enabled him to complete a full day's work in each city. He did his best to fit his London engagements into consecutive days: of these, by far the most important was the Top Salaries Review Body, of which he was appointed chairman in 1971. This was a major commitment which at first he was reluctant to take on, knowing the full-time nature of his job as Vice-Chancellor. He was persuaded to do so by the Prime Minister, and for ten years (he resigned the chair not long before his death) it remained his most important task outside the University. The setting of 'top' salaries in the public sector was a most sensitive issue; Jean Orr explains the nature of the work and describes the recommendations made in one of the areas reviewed, that of parliamentary pay. The Review Body met once a fortnight throughout the year (and more frequently before the submission of a report) and apart from his University commitments these meetings took precedence in Edward's life over all other engagements. As to his success in chairing the Review Body, it is notable that at every change of government he was asked to continue the work: he held the confidence of four such different Prime Ministers as Edward Heath (who appointed him), Harold Wilson, James Callaghan and Margaret Thatcher.

One appointment which took Edward abroad at this time was as UK representative – one of two – to the European University Institute at Florence. He enjoyed these visits and his discussions with the director, while appreciating the fine position of the Institute in the hills of Fiesole. Of all his appointments, however, the one which gave him most pleasure was the trusteeship of the British Museum, to which he was appointed by Harold Wilson in 1970. The meetings being held on a Saturday morning enabled him to come from Leeds, overnight if necessary, and he took considerable trouble not to miss them. He served on the education and the staff committees, and took as his special area of interest (as a trustee was required to do) the department of Egyptian antiquities. In 1980, the first year of his illness, he was re-appointed to serve a further term, and this pleased him more than any other event that year.

Edward's musical interests were well catered for in Yorkshire, where he found much to enjoy in the University itself, in the city of Leeds where he was an active president of the Leeds Festival Club, and at the Harrogate festival. A particular pleasure was his involvement with the Leeds piano competition, and he was delighted and gratified to be invited to act as chairman of the jury in 1972, as Fanny Waterman describes.

Always an eager party giver, in 1973 he gave the most splendid of all his parties. It was the year of his own 50th birthday, of his sister Ann Gold and her husband's silver wedding and of his niece Georgina's 21st birthday. It seemed to him a year for a particularly glorious celebration and he knew exactly what sort of party he would like to give. He had long admired the singer Elisabeth Schwarzkopf for her interpretation of *lieder* and was delighted when she agreed to give a recital with Gerald Moore; he was especially pleased that she was willing to consider his own requests for the programme. As Alexander Goehr suspects, Edward had a considerable hand in the planning of the programme and he later treasured the letters he received from Walter Legge discussing its content, of which the second half was devoted to Hugo Wolf; Edward himself wrote programme notes for each song. The recital was given at the Hyde Park Hotel, and followed by a supper, and Edward generously let the Golds choose half the guests.

Edward was invited to give the 1977 BBC Reith lectures and to speak on the subject of British political institutions. He planned to immerse himself in the subject for a short period and he hoped, too, to have an opportunity for discussion and exchange of ideas with those at the centre of political life in London. He never found time for this, and although he did some preliminary reading he did not find sufficient time to cover the ground and prepare the lectures, so that in the end and to his great regret he was obliged to withdraw. Another commission was a BBC guide to the music of Fauré, which he undertook in 1974. In this case Edward collected musical material and gave several talks on the composer, but postponed the writing of the book.

Edward was always loth to acknowledge personal ill-health; he grew up with a certain feeling of guilt about claiming to be unwell, and this, together with an enthusiasm for whatever he was doing which tended to mask natural feelings of fatigue, led to his doing too much by normal standards. He anticipated that he might, later in life, be affected by the same sort of heart problems as his father and grandmother, but cancer was unknown in the family. It was therefore a particular shock to him to find himself already badly affected by cancer in the autumn of 1979.

His case was taken up personally by the Professor of Medicine at the University, and from thenceforward he received all the help the medical school could supply. He spent some time in both of the University teaching hospitals, the Leeds General Infirmary and St James's, and the feeling that he was now getting to know the hospitals from the inside whereas hitherto his concern with them as Vice-Chancellor had been only from the outside gave him a small sense of satisfaction. His initial operation to halt the spread of symptoms was successful, and he was able to continue with all his University duties and many of his additional activities, including the Top Salaries Review Body. He had an optimistic feeling that the skills of the doctors and staff of the Leeds University Medical School had been sufficient to restore to him a tolerably normal working life, even if it could not be such an arduous one as before. He co-operated with the medical authorities to the greatest extent, carefully studying his X-ray pictures and diligently following advice about methods of losing weight in order to put less strain on his now fragile bones. In the loss of weight he was spectacularly successful, quickly learning the exact number of calories in every item and quantity of food, so that many were shocked by the change in his appearance which was quite startling.

The second year of his illness started with a straightforward operation to pin a fragile leg-bone; Edward made heroic efforts to learn to walk again after falling down and bending the pin, taking infinite pains to move his crutches in accordance with the theory which had been explained to him. He returned to his duties at the University and travelled as usual to London and elsewhere for meetings, though during the course of the year he became increasingly frail.

In June 1981 Edward was made a Companion of Honour and this award gave him real pleasure: he felt grateful and proud to be invited to join such a distinguished company of former recipients. It also brought him 300 letters of congratulation. A capacity for enjoying himself was one of Edward's most marked characteristics, so that even at this stage he greatly enjoyed receiving this final mixed postbag, the details of which - the names, the order of arrival, the contents - he later reported to his sister from memory.

At the end of July Edward came to London with a typically busy programme: he had engagements all day for five days and dinner engagements every night. By now he was exceedingly thin and found difficulty in walking, but he got along at a reasonable pace using a stick and he went about as unselfconsciously and eagerly as ever.

One of those whom he saw at this time was the Prime Minister, who had recommended him for the C.H. award and who, knowing of his declining health, asked him now to come to Downing Street. Edward and Margaret Thatcher had been on friendly terms since their Oxford days, when both were active in the University Conservative Association. On this occasion (according to Edward) she was 'very warm, very solicitous'; however, after a generous period of kindly talk and affectionate enquiry she paused and pulled up her chair: 'Now, Edward,' she said more briskly, 'about the universities . . . ' Edward thought it sensible of her to take what would obviously be her last opportunity of picking his brains, and he set about answering her questions as helpfully as he could.

Edward followed the course of his illness with an intellectual interest, carefully learning the names of new drugs and anticipating their effects. He did not complain, but as he became weaker his expression showed the conflict in his mind: between, on the one hand, his effort to accept what his reason told him about the certainty of his approaching death and on the other, his difficulty in disengaging himself from the huge range of issues and interests about which he cared deeply and for which he passionately wanted to live. His illness never affected his mind and he set himself certain targets: the last one which he achieved was to attend the wedding of his niece Georgina, as she describes. He returned to Leeds for another three weeks after the wedding, though unable to attend the finals of the Leeds piano competition as he had hoped, and he died at the Lodge on 28 September, aged 58.

The family funeral was at Salehurst in Sussex where he was buried beside his parents and grandparents. Edward often took Ockham visitors for a walk to Salehurst, where the handsome abbey church stands at the corner of a quiet lane, flanked by hop-fields. He liked to show people the substantial memorial to Lord Milner which lies on the opposite side of the graveyard from the Boyle plot. Though totally different in background and beliefs, Edward and Lord Milner do have one similarity to justify the coincidence of their both lying in the same small, rather isolated churchyard: both were unconventional members of the Conservative Party who believed that the public good is of greater importance than party dogma. More than that, they both had considerable power to attract others to their ideas, even across party lines, and to influence the thinking of younger men looking towards similar public-spirited goals.

Public tributes followed the family funeral: firstly a memorial service in the Great Hall of Leeds University, at which the pianist Murray Perahia played the piece for which Edward had specially asked, as Fanny Waterman explains. In October a fine service was held at St Margaret's, Westminster, for which Edward Heath chose the music and gave the address. In November, William Walsh gave the address at a memorial service in Leeds Parish church. A few weeks later a trust was established in Edward's name to promote excellence in three areas of special interest to him: education, learning and music. With the Chancellor of Leeds University, H.R.H. The Duchess of Kent, as patron of the trust, 40 people of great distinction in public life and of varying political views lent their support as vice-patrons, and the inaugural address was given by Harold Macmillan.

It is unusual for a man who has achieved only moderate advancement in political and public life – Edward held only one Cabinet office – to be so much honoured publicly when he dies. The purpose of this book is to examine the reasons behind this by observing Edward through the eyes of many different people. This introductory summary of the circumstances and events of his life is followed now by a series of personal recollections, each one illustrating some aspect of that life well-known to the writer.

In Edward's case, his influence cannot be assessed simply by examining his record in the offices he held: it is something less tangible, an influence for good among those whom he knew and those with whom he worked in a crowded life. For this reason the story of his life needs contributions by many people, which together may form a comprehensive picture of the man and illustrate those distinctive qualities which made his personality unique.

Introduction 47

Notes

1. Professor Michael Jaffé, Director, Fitzwilliam Museum, 1973–89. From 'The kindness of a Tory intellectual', *Sunday Telegraph*, 4.10.81.
2. Sir Edward Boyle, first baronet, 1848–1909.
3. Sir Edward Boyle, second baronet, 1878–1945.
4. *The Times*, 3.4.45.
5. It is not known whether the picture is still there.
6. From an unpublished memoir written for the family by Edward's father in 1934.
7. From 'A Classical Education Revisited'. Presidential address delivered to the Classical Association in the University of Lancaster, 17.4.73.
8. Michael Hughes-Hallett. He was 14 when he fagged for Edward, who was 17.
9. Letter to Edward's father, 9.8.42.
10. W. J. Owen, who held the rank of Captain (later Major) at Bletchley, where he came in 1943. Letter 16.11.88.
11. Sir Thomas Armstrong, FRCM. Organist of Christ Church, Oxford 1933–55. Principal, Royal Academy of Music, 1955–68. Letter 12.1.89.
12. From Edward's 1955 Election Address.
13. Edward's own description in a letter of 1.5.63.
14. July 1954.
15. 28.12.55.
16. Written 26.12.88 by Michael Hall, son of Alderman F. T. D. Hall, Chairman of the Handsworth Conservative and Unionist Association 1965–73.
17. Letter to W. J. Owen, 5.2.57.
18. From Edward's 1959 Election Address.
19. Kaye Webb, MBE. Editor, Puffin Books and Publishing Director children's Division, Penguin Books, 1961–79. Letter 4.7.89.
20. *Guardian*, 4.7.72.
21. Mrs Marjorie Austin, an officer of the Handsworth Conservative and Unionist Association. Letter, 1.11.88.
22. Professor Sir Roy Marshall, Secretary-General, Committee of Vice-Chancellors and Principals, 1974–79.
23. The Alfred Mays lecture, 1976: 'Parliament's views on responsibility for education policy since 1944', pub. Institute of Local Government Studies, University of Birmingham.
24. From 'Karl Popper's Open Society: a personal appreciation', manuscript 1971. This article pub. in *The Philosophy of Karl Popper*, ed. Paul A. Schilpp, 1974.

2

Edward at Home
Elizabeth Longford

The Boyle family lived at Ockham, Hurst Green, East Sussex. They had been close neighbours of the Pakenhams at Bernhurst since time immemorial – or so it has always seemed to me. I first met Edward's elegant mother, Lady (Beatrice) Boyle in the early 1930s. She was a friend of my husband Frank's great-aunt Caroline Pakenham, the chatelaine of Bernhurst until she died in 1938 aged 96 and her great–nephew Frank inherited it. I remember visiting Great-Aunt Caroline soon after we married in 1931 and having tea with her and Beatrice Boyle in the revolving summerhouse on the lawn. The widowed Aunt Caroline, always dressed in black, a replica of Queen Victoria, insisted on making our tea herself from a silver tea–kettle with a fifty-yard-long flex plugged into the butler's pantry indoors. Beatrice and I exchanged smiles at this lengthy 'modern' procedure, the kettle having been intended for a spirit lamp, not electricity.

My first memory of young Edward (his father, Sir Edward Boyle, was still alive) turned out to be an appropriately vivid political one. It was a summer day in 1939. We younger ones were all playing tennis on the court at Ockham that lay back to the left at the bottom of the long descending drive. Beyond the tennis-court was a 'deep dark dell' surrounded by oak trees and filled with flowering shrubs; beyond that the house, a Jacobean-style brick mansion enlarged for his family by Edward's father.

The standard of play on the tennis–court that day was not high, for everyone was excited and agitated. But the agitation inside the house was far greater. For news had come through that Mussolini had invaded Albania and Edward's father was the acknowledged expert on that country's past and present.

Would the great man be urgently summoned by the Chamberlain government for consultation and advice or would they ignore his expertise? Perish the thought!

At last, I think after tea, the long-expected telephone call came through from Downing Street, Sir Edward was sent for to No. 10 and tension at Ockham temporarily relaxed.

Young Edward, still a schoolboy at Eton, was left to play the host in his father's place. And most admirably did he fill the role. We had all gathered in the comfortable library and talk, of course, was of Albania, its little known past history and perilous future. Suddenly young Edward took over. To everyone's amazement he put us into the Albanian picture with an unexampled virtuosity. He seemed to know every bit as much about the situation as his revered father, and concluded his brilliant little disquisition with a recital of the relevant royal houses from medieval times to the present day. In my mind, I marked him up as a future politician or academic of the utmost charm, brilliance and enthusiasm.

The invasion of Albania was soon to be revealed as one of the dictators' preliminary 'strikes' before the Second World War broke out in September 1939. From 1940 to 1945 the Boyles of Ockham and Pakenhams of Bernhurst had no contact, though their respective homes contributed in various picturesque ways to the 'war effort'. Edward had meanwhile left Eton where he had been very popular and acquired life-long friends. One aspect of Edward's popularity as a schoolboy polymath was disclosed to me only many years later, when village cricket was again in full force at Hurst Green after the war. He attended matches whenever possible and cricket was one of the many subjects about which Edward knew everything that there was to know. I was told by an admirer that though he seldom played the game himself at Eton, his knowledge, resourcefulness and interest in it were such that he was appointed the college's official cricket scorer – quite a considerable compliment to a virtual non-player!

Having left Eton, Edward did secret work at Bletchley during the war, while Ockham was taken over by the government and filled with troops. At the very beginning of the war, while the family were still there, it received evacuees, one of whom was a young redhead called Ruth Williams. Here another link was to be established between us and Edward. Years later Frank and I were to invite Ruth, her African husband Seretse Khama, ruler of Botswana, and two babies to lunch with us in Cheyne Gardens, Chelsea, where Ruth was soon telling us about her temporary billet at Ockham as a schoolgirl and how much she had enjoyed her stay in Sir Edward Boyle's home. (By this time Edward was a prominent MP with a great interest in the

Commonwealth and much sympathy with the plight of blacks.)

Ockham was surrounded by woods and fields and felt far removed from the main A21 road, though in fact it was quite close. In front of the house was a broad terrace running the whole length and facing south, to a magnificent view over the next village of Robertsbridge and the Sussex countryside between the village and the sea. The sea was only about 12 miles away and one somehow sensed it in the light and air of Ockham. Below the terrace was a wide lawn ending in a steep, wooded drop, with a lily-and-goldfish pool in the lawn's centre. I never saw the kitchen garden, but there must have been a fine one, judging by the delicious vegetables we were to consume at Edward's hospitable table after the war.

At the same time that Ockham was being used by the Army, Bernhurst was contributing in its own way to the war effort. It, too, was taken over by the government. (Our family were living in Oxford.) A group of officers inhabited the house, soldiers were housed in huts on the lawn and lorries parked in the orchard.

It was in the first new decade after the war – the formidable fifties – that I really got to know Edward well as a noble human being and most high-minded statesman. While Beatrice Boyle his mother was alive she was of course hostess at Ockham; after her death it was sometimes his sister Ann, editor of this book and wife of the architect Jack Gold. Their children, Jason and Georgina, were to represent 'youth' at the heart of Edward's family, and therefore, to him, priceless treasures.

I nearly always talked politics with Edward at his parties, and politics equally dominated his visits to Bernhurst. I daresay he would also have talked music to us, if Frank and I had been capable of it. Unfortunately we were not. However, we were well aware of the supreme part that music played at Ockham, through Beatrice, a cellist, through his mother's great friends and frequent visitors Adila Fachiri and Jelly d'Aranyi, the famous violinists, and through young Edward himself. Greatly daring, I once asked Edward if he had ever been in love. He said: Yes, when he was a boy, with Jelly d'Aranyi. From the way he said it, I could see that this had been literally a consuming passion and had consumed once for all the fuel that otherwise might have fed other loves. I may have been wrong, but this is what I felt.

I can remember a talk with Edward in the early 1950s about the pleasures of being Economic Secretary to the Treasury, an impressive position that he had achieved in 1955 at the age of 31. He was about to represent his country at a conference in Istanbul, and already knew all about Byzantine history and art, as well as the world's monetary problems. His shining pink cheeks and sparkling blue eyes, not to mention his characteristic rush of eager conversation when breaths had to be snatched as if they were his last, made me realise how deeply he was looking forward to this new political experience. That in turn was later to impress on me the extent of his sacrifice in resigning over Suez.

Frank will never forget how Edward broke to him his decision to resign; his rapid speech yet soft undertone conveying both the certainty that he was doing right and a kind of awe at the seriousness of such action: 'I've got to go out on this one . . . '

We happened to be visiting our third son Michael at Ampleforth College during the 'Suez weekend' after Edward's resignation. We found that Michael's housemaster and many another of Ampleforth's Catholic monks treated Edward with an acclaim that was only this side of idolatry, for his courage, the dignity of his resignation and his choice of the *right* rather than the *expedient*. We soon realised the gravity of his action in resigning. In subsequent weekends at Bernhurst we learnt that the Sunday *Observer*, edited by David Astor, which bravely supported Boyle and denounced Eden – its leading article was entitled 'Eden' – suffered a catastrophic fall in circulation.

Our eldest son, Thomas Pakenham, has a lively recollection of a conversation with Edward at Ockham during the period when he was a 'fallen minister'. Ockham, as I have said, was rich in fields and woods which themselves were over-rich in pigeons. One Friday evening Thomas called on Edward to ask if he might shoot pigeons on the Ockham estate - Bernhurst fields being temporarily free of them. Edward, who was about ten years older than Thomas, drew his young guest into his small sanctum that led out of the large library. Immediately they were immersed in political discussion. Gradually Thomas became aware that he was talking to no 'true blue Tory' in the narrow accepted sense but to a statesman to whom international law and order, breached by the Suez fiasco, meant more than his own career.

'Why are you a member of that party?' Thomas eventually found himself asking Edward. (He and his parents were Labour.)

'I am not an undifferentiated Tory,' admitted Boyle. There were in fact to be four questions on which Edward would find himself in disagreement with 'true blue Toryism': Suez, the blacks, legislation concerning homosexuals, and capital punishment. Frank and I have always realised, however, that had Edward joined the Labour Party, he would have eventually found at least two obstacles in his path: anti-nuclearism and collectivism. He would have made a very good Liberal.

Thomas remembers his going on to ask Edward whether he preferred Tories who had 'risen from the working-class or lower middle-classes' to those from the higher reaches of society. 'Oh no, they are far too deferential; cap-touching,' said Edward. The most unsnobbish of men, he could not bear people paying homage to his rank – a hereditary baronetcy.

That first conversation at Ockham, which was meant to be entirely about pigeons, led to other interesting meetings. Thomas remained always faintly in awe of Edward the polymath – 'His depth and width of knowledge were truly awe inspiring, he would have been a sure winner in Mastermind' – while Edward's kindness was based on the Ockham connection twinned with his pleasure in the company of youth. Thomas remembers one occasion when they met accidentally near the Carlton Club and Edward took him inside for a drink. 'Soon he was burbling away in his typical polysyllabic manner, trying to draw one out; to get at one's own ideas. Edward *never* went on talking for its own sake. It was always to bring out whoever he was talking to.'

The most exciting time when Thomas enjoyed one of those uncovenanted dialogues was on the way to a conference of the National Union of Teachers which Edward, as Minister of Education and in the Cabinet, was going to address. Catching sight of Thomas on the train, he invited the cub reporter on education into his carriage. The memory of their conversation has always remained with him, partly because he was so much flattered to be singled out by the great minister, chiefly because of Edward's strongly expressed views on a certain topical problem. A woman teacher had been sacked on the grounds of her unsuitable private life. Asked his opinion on the question, Edward gave a forthright reply. 'I only consider two things in such cases: Does it damage anyone else? Is it a joyous and life-enhancing experience?'

Edward's appointment as Parliamentary Secretary to the Ministry of Education after his Suez resignation was something of a joyous surprise to his friends; even more so to himself. He told Frank that he had been astonished when Harold Macmillan asked him to dinner in order to offer him a post in his government. Macmillan has been described as 'first in' and 'first out' over Suez - in fact he was a Suez man.

Moreover, after Eden's breakdown and resignation, Edward had not been among Macmillan's supporters for the premiership. 'Actually I wanted Rab as PM,' he told me, as I congratulated him on his excellent new job, during a Sussex weekend.

I could always understand without difficulty why Edward backed Rab. 'The art of the possible' was Rab's motto in politics – an art which automatically ruled out all political extremes, such as jingoism, aggression or the belief that in foreign as in home affairs the slogan should be 'might is right' and 'devil take the hindmost'. Harold Macmillan, fortunately, was also to practise an art very acceptable to Edward when he annunciated the 'Wind of Change' in Africa.

I have many poignant memories of Edward's last years at Ockham. Gatherings on the terrace acquired a new vitality when Georgina and Jason were present, or when the glorious banksia rose was in flower, shedding a primrose light all over the front of the house.

When Thomas married Valerie McNair-Scott in 1964, Edward asked them to Ockham to celebrate with champagne and the playing of his most treasured record: 'The Coronation of Poppaea' by Monteverdi. We detected a joke in the fact that the lovely Poppaea was crowned on her marriage – to the Emperor Nero!

My last memory of Edward at Ockham was when he came over to dinner with us at Bernhurst for my birthday, loaded with a superb print of Queen Victoria and John Brown. It is four feet long, from the painting by Edwin Landseer. The old Queen, seated on a shining pony, is reading her dispatches while the kilted ghillie holds the pony. Today the picture is the first one sees on entering Bernhurst.

I felt that Edward's decision to leave Parliament and Ockham for Leeds and the University Vice-Chancellorship was the right one. His deep dedication to the cause of youth and learning was henceforth to take a more practical and intimate shape. He once very kindly came to the reception before a literary lunch I was to address in Leeds. He was clearly ill and failing but looked happy. Afterwards I asked a common friend how Edward managed to avoid the worst of the student troubles that were then prevalent.

'He is always there, among us,' was the convincing reply. 'If you go to lunch in the refectory you are more than likely to see Edward slip unobtrusively into an empty seat and begin a meal and conversation with the students round the table. He knows what everyone is thinking. He is never out of touch.'

Though we realised that his Leeds decision to leave his Sussex home was fully justified, he was widely missed at Hurst Green, the village where his family had lived for so many years. Edward had the gift of supporting with patent sincerity good causes in which he could not personally believe but which he recognised as essential parts of village life. He was understood to have lost his faith. But this did not prevent him from supporting the village church and opening and attending fêtes in aid of our small new Catholic church – from whose dogmas he was even more remote than those of Anglicanism. His butler, Denis, was a kind of 'Admirable Crichton', a devoted servant to the family and also a devoted son of the Catholic Church who would spend his summer holiday from Ockham as a stretcher-bearer at Lourdes. Denis was always aware of Edward's unique form of sympathy for other people's beliefs.

Edward was a great mixer. One weekend he would be entertaining old friends from the Cabinet or Opposition at Ockham; the next, supping with the village schoolmaster and schoolmistress, where we were made to tell stories or listen to theirs: how the bee-keeping schoolmaster once got a bee up his trousers; or how the parson's wife dreamt she was arrested for stealing from Woolworth's.

Edward was perhaps too good to climb to the top in politics, but he reached a better summit in people's hearts. I am sure the poet Browning's works were in the Ockham library, and I am sure that he had read them. At any rate, the following lines from Browning have always seemed to Frank and myself touchingly appropriate to the memory of Edward Boyle.

> Lofty designs must close in like effects,
>   Loftily lying,
> Leave him still loftier than the world suspects,
>   Living and dying.

I hope and believe that this book will make 'the world' more fully aware not only of Edward's 'lofty designs' but also of his noble achievements.

3

At Preparatory School
Michael Howard

On a fine afternoon in May 1933 I took Edward for a walk round the school grounds at Abinger Hill, where he had just arrived as a new boy. I was ten, he nine, and since I was a year senior to him in the school I had been deputed to act as his 'Big Brother'. The spring sunshine shone through the unfolding leaves, the birds sang cheerfully, and Edward explained to me in some detail the structure of Elgar's cello concerto.

That set the pattern of our relationship – and I suspect the relationship between Edward and many other people – for the next forty years. I knew what a cello was, but I was by no means sure about concertos and certainly had never heard of Elgar. I did not dare say so because I was afraid that Edward would not believe me. He took it for granted that everyone was as well informed as he, and dealt with them accordingly. It was probably the wisest course: the only alternatives, certainly at Abinger and probably everywhere else, would have been either to turn every conversation into a tutorial or to abstain from any dialogue at all. As it was, I went away and learned about Elgar. A year or so later Edward asked me to name my favourite composer, and on the strength of the *Ständchen* (which I had just heard for the first time) I replied, Schubert. Edward (now aged ten) gave guarded approval: Schubert's quartets, he granted, were indeed remarkable. But on the grounds of sheer range and brilliance he preferred Mozart, especially some of his later choral works. And so it went on. Whenever we met in later life a name would come up, whether of a musician or a statesman or a philosopher, on the fringe of my knowledge if not beyond it, which Edward would discuss as if I had just written the definitive monograph on the topic. I need hardly add that on subjects which I did know something about, Edward always knew considerably more.

But I did not mind. Although it was sometimes heavy going, one could not resent Edward's superiority, because he was genuinely superior. Further, there was never in his character the slightest trace of pretentiousness or arrogance. He dealt with everyone as if they were his equals and listened to their opinions with respect. While he often made me feel ill-informed, he never made anyone feel, or look, *stupid*. As a result he was regarded at Abinger with a mixture of awe and affection that made him one of the most popular boys in the school.

Abinger was, admittedly, a rather exceptional place which attracted rather exceptional boys – or rather the sons of rather exceptional parents. Professor Julian Huxley, Sir Oswald Mosley, Sir Robert Mayer, Lord Melchett and Montague Norman were only some of the more glamorous figures who came down on parents' week–ends. The grounds sprawled over the southern slopes of Leith Hill, restrictions were minimal and boys were treated as early as feasible in their careers as intelligent if eccentric adults by a staff, none of whom were over forty and most considerably younger. Work was flexibly arranged to allow for the greatest amount of diversity and initiative. Formal instruction was kept to the minimum, and extra-curricular activities almost swamped curricular. In the summer we slept out in the woods, learning woodcraft skills, studying plant or animal life, or more often waging prolonged guerrilla campaigns. We mounted open-air plays and pageants, inspired and at times assisted by our illustrious neighbours Vaughan Williams and E. M. Forster. In the winter we held vigorous debates, wrote and produced plays, organised concerts and film shows, held mock-elections and mock trials and scribbled verse and short stories for the school magazine. If you were not good at orthodox games – and Edward's globular shape discommoded him from most of them – there were plenty of other activities at which you could shine. If you were good at work – and in this respect Edward far out-soared the shadow of our night – it showed up not in invidious competition with others but in a record of individual performance week by week which, if sufficiently remarkable, earned the whole school a quarter-holiday. Quarter-holidays rained down when Edward was around like Danae's golden shower.

It was difficult to think of Edward as ever being young. Rather he was like Mr Bultitude in F. Anstey's *Vice Versa* in which the unfortunate 40-year-old hero finds himself trapped in the body of a 12-year-old schoolboy. But Edward, unlike Mr Bultitude, managed his predicament with great skill. He floundered happily and ruefully at the end of organised runs. He got stuck in the obstacles in obstacle races. He developed a revolting but hugely popular parlour trick which consisted in folding his capacious belly into a kind of marsupial pouch and lapping out of it the milk we had to drink for elevenses. His vast learning and academic skills were at the service of any boy who cared to use them. And, though useless on the cricket field, he became a highly professional scorer and expert on the history and intricacies of the game, knowing Wisden backwards by the age of 12. His precocity was thus cheerfully placed at the service of the common weal, in childhood as it was to be in later life.

We were much thrown together by our tastes, interests and inaptitude for organised games. Our friendship was made closer by the fact that we lived within walking distance of each other in South Kensington and spent much of the holidays playing gramophone records together and going to concerts at the Albert Hall. Back at school we collaborated in running the school magazine, producing plays and, in 1935, organising a mock election. Edward affectionately and with typical self–mockery called our partnership that of an Elephant and Howdah, and we fed each other's precocity as little boys will. In only one field, however, was I really able to compete. Reading the school magazine for summer 1936, our final term, I discover that in that year we both competed for the Townsend-Warner History Prize for preparatory schools, and that out of 76 entries Edward came third in the 'facts' paper and in the 'essay' paper I came first. Quite right too. God only knows how I did on the 'facts' paper, but that is an ancillary aspect of historical study which I have never taken very seriously.

Our paths then separated and nearly a decade passed before we met again. I went to Wellington, a musical as well as a military school, and Edward to Eton, where he no doubt found himself less intellectually isolated than at Abinger. Wellington probably modified my precocity as much as Eton intensified Edward's; and our different experience of war service, mine with an infantry battalion in Italy and Edward's at the intellectual hub of the war effort at Bletchley Park, completed the process of turning us into very different kinds of people. We both went up to Oxford in autumn 1945. Although my ambitions were still academic, I had acquired worldly and frivolous tastes, whereas Edward had put away childish things and matured into a deeply serious intellectual heavyweight, more at home with people twice his age than with other undergraduates. His interests had deepened and narrowed, focusing on the philosophy of R. G. Collingwood, the economic theory of Maynard Keynes and – a pleasing eccentricity – Victorian church music. If one could not keep up with him in these fields – as quite frankly I could not – conversation tended to fall off. In any case his eyes were now set on the political heights, and much of his time at Oxford was spent at the Union and elsewhere preparing himself to scale them. This combination of a highly idiosyncratic intellectual diet and increasing involvement in the world of affairs may have resulted in a lack of concentration on the immediate demands of the Oxford History School and explained why, to the amazement of all his contemporaries, he only obtained a third-class Honours degree.

How deeply this affected Edward himself I do not know; but as someone who himself got a rather bad second I know how badly this might shake someone with a good conceit of himself. Certainly Edward was a serious historian and loved the subject. Whenever we met thereafter he showed – and was perhaps at pains to show – how well he had kept up with his reading and how familiar he was with the latest scholarly articles. It was in the realization that he still retained an appetite for academic affairs beyond that of the average Secretary of State for Education that led me in the mid-1960s, when I was on the search committee for the Principalship of King's College, London, to cast a fly over Edward and see if he was attracted by the prospect of returning to academic life. He responded more eagerly than I had expected, but the time was not ripe. He was not yet quite ready to leave political life: perhaps the Chancellorship of the Exchequer still beckoned. So London missed him, and a few years later Leeds reaped the benefit.

Lucky Leeds. His achievement there was enormous. And I have no doubt that on Sunday afternoons he would take favoured undergraduates for walks round the campus, explaining to them at a rather deeper level of analysis the structure of Elgar's cello concerto; much as he had done to me, forty years before.

4

Eton and Early Politics
John Grigg

Edward Boyle and I were not exact contemporaries at Eton, but near enough. He was eight months older and so, I think, came to the school a term or two before I did. Certainly he was my immediate predecessor as Captain of the Oppidans (as the head of the school, apart from the Collegers, is called). But we got to know each other very well half way through our time, after we had taken School Certificate and become history specialists. For the three years before he left in the summer of 1942 we met as a rule several times a day at work, while the greater freedom that went with being specialists enabled us also to meet a lot out of school hours. Thus was formed a friendship that lasted until his wretchedly premature death forty years later.

We were not in the same house, but used to visit each other's rooms 'after twelve' (the period of leisure between the end of morning school and lunch), on half-holiday afternoons, or during summer evenings when houses stayed open later – not to mention Sundays. Edward knew far more than I did about most subjects of which I had any knowledge at all, and his range of knowledge extended to subjects with which I was totally unacquainted. But I had one asset: my father, Edward Grigg, was a minister in Churchill's government, and through him I was aware of what was happening in the world of politics. Indeed I was obsessively interested in the subject, as Edward was, too, though without having been brought up in quite such a political atmosphere as I had. In retrospect, it seems that I may have been able to give him an early, if vicarious, sense of the exciting world in which most of his career was to be spent, and towards which his talents already beckoned.

What he gave me in return – as well as the sheer pleasure of his company – was the privilege of communing with one of the finest intellects of our generation. It was not just the amount he knew, but the feeling he unselfconsciously conveyed of having known it all from time immemorial, and of having reflected deeply on almost any topic one might raise. A favourite phrase of his was 'I have *always* thought that . . . ', and even when he was 16 it seemed literally true. How could he ever have been ignorant or immature?

Yet he was not only very young, but also in some ways acutely vulnerable. His rotund shape and bubbling good nature misled many who knew him only casually into assuming that he was at ease with life. In fact, like Dr Johnson, he was a mass of nerves. His finger-nails were bitten to the quick, and he seldom sat still. As we talked in his room at Eton, he would more often than not be throwing a cricket ball rapidly from hand to hand. The combination of mental precocity and physical oddity imposed a considerable strain on him, which insensitive treatment tended to aggravate. He did not wish to be regarded as a freak, but was too often made to feel one. His housemaster, C. R. N. Routh, who was also a history master, would refer to him facetiously in class as 'Professor Boyle', and did not appoint him head of the house even when he was Captain of the Oppidans – rather as Sir Leonard Hutton was later denied the captaincy of Yorkshire while he had that of England. Beyond question Edward was hurt at being passed over, though he pretended not to be. The implication that he had an overdeveloped brain but no practical ability secretly rankled.

Among his contemporaries he was almost universally popular, though the attitude of many of them towards him was not unlike Mr Routh's, in that they were apt to regard him as a 'character' whose intellectual virtuosity, like his physique, was somehow quaint and funny. In a community where athletic prowess was paramount he was at an obvious disadvantage, but did not compound this by showing any lack of respect for athletes. On the contrary, his genuine interest in games was reassuring to them, and boosted their self-esteem. Above all, his love of cricket and cricketing lore appealed to the cricketers, to the extent that as scorer to the XI he was awarded a cap and became a sort of mascot. His own games–playing activities brought him little satisfaction, though in winter he did take part in the school's peculiar variety of football, and in our last summer was my partner in the school tennis competition, when we managed to get through two rounds. Later, tennis metaphors came naturally to him, as when he remarked to me of Anthony Eden that, as a parliamentary debater, he could 'hit the ball exceptionally hard and low across the net'.

Edward's own formidable talent for debate found an outlet at Eton when, in 1939, a school debating society was started on the initiative of Adrian Liddell Hart and Roger Spicer, with Edward and myself among the original members. The society met in a small annexe of school library, under the chairmanship of a kindly paraplegic, Mr McMaster, but with boys largely controlling the programme. Adrian Liddell Hart reminds me that in October 1939 he proposed a motion calling for immediate peace with Germany, which Edward and I opposed, and which (I am glad to say) was lost. The headmaster, Claude Elliott, was consulted about the motion in advance but did not prohibit its discussion, which in the circumstances was astonishing: all the more so as he was a very cautious man, to whom debating at the best of times was a suspect form of activity. Very different was the provost, Lord Quickswood, who as Lord Hugh Cecil had in his day been one of the best speakers in the House of Commons. Argument was the breath of life to him and he was easily persuaded to visit the society on more than one occasion.

At every meeting Edward's intervention was likely to be the star turn. His style was never rhetorical, but he spoke with wonderful fluency and with a range of allusion that none could match. It was the same style, personal to himself, that he later employed in the Oxford Union and in Parliament. Though his precise line of argument was seldom predictable, one could be sure that he would speak in the name of reason and give short shrift to any excesses of emotion or idealism. He would often take a studiedly worldly line as, for instance, when he proposed, in February 1942, 'that the true politician is not a gentleman', arguing that progress was more or less automatic, political idealism therefore unnecessary, and opportunism, even caddishness, the appropriate attributes of a politician. Nobody could have guessed, at that stage of his life, that only 14 years later he would resign office and risk the total extinction of a bright career for the sake of principle.

His attitude to religion was, at the time, equally sceptical. I well remember him reading me I Corinthians 15, verses 12–14: 'Now if Christ be preached that he rose from the dead, how say some among you that there is no resurrection of the dead? But if there be no resurrection of the dead, then is Christ not risen: And if Christ be not risen, then is our preaching vain, and your faith is also vain.' His comment on this text, delivered to the accompaniment of hands thumped together, was: 'That has *always* seemed to me the perfect example of a circular argument.' Not for him then, or perhaps ever, the illogical and selective approach of the average English Christian. To him, Christianity was a package which had either to be accepted in its entirety as an act of faith, or wholly rejected as an affront to reason.

His aesthetic sense was, of course, supremely evident in his passion for music. This I shared, though at a much lower level of experience and comprehension. While I was wallowing in the more obvious masterpieces of Bach, Handel, Mozart, Beethoven, Chopin or Wagner, with which he had been familiar for so long that he took them for granted, he would prefer to talk about lesser-known – and to me usually unknown – works of such masters, or about composers of whom I had as yet heard nothing, such as Mahler or Schoenberg.

Visually he was less of an aesthete: indeed, if one were to judge by his room in Mr Routh's house, he was scarcely a visual aesthete at all. The house itself was dingy, and the rooms lacked the variety of shape and character that could be found in older houses. But it is always possible to give some personal atmosphere, even a little charm, to the most unpromising room, and this Edward failed to do. For a person of such very marked individuality his room was strangely impersonal; and this was true not only at Eton but throughout his life. Yet in certain ways he did have an eye for beauty, and it was, as one might expect, an independent eye. In particular, he did not join in the then fashionable condemnation of Victorian architecture, but much admired the work of, for instance, Butterfield. His taste for Victorian buildings anticipated the Betjeman-led change of sensibility in the post-war world.

It should not for a moment be thought that our talk at Eton was all to do with politics, religion or the arts. Much of it – probably most of it – took the form of gossip, which Edward always enjoyed. His subtle interest in people made him the greatest fun to talk to about mutual friends and acquaintances. Though without malice, he was sharply observant of human foibles; his benevolence was never of the sloppy kind. By the same token his criticisms of people were always measured, and he reacted instinctively against any sign of intolerance, however petty. Some years later, when we were both lunching with Jakie Astor, a Labour MP also present said of a colleague that he was the sort of person who would go to a film in the afternoon. Amid laughter at the man's expense, Edward turned to me and asked *sotto voce* 'Why shouldn't he go to a film in the afternoon?' The unconventional and truly liberal spirit of this question was fully apparent at Eton.

For the next two years we hardly met. He was at Bletchley, and I (after leaving Eton in early 1943) in the Army, for part of the time abroad. Moreover, he was never a good correspondent, preferring to meet or talk on the telephone. But on 9 September 1945 he wrote me a long letter from Bedford, in reply to one from me commiserating with him on the death of his father. At the same time he sent me a copy of his father's *Biographical Essays 1790–1890* (a delightful collection, by the way, which deserves to be reprinted). But most of the letter was devoted to the recent general election, and as evidence of his attitude at the time to the Conservative Party and politics generally it seems worth quoting at some length.

A mutual friend had told me that he (Edward) had been active in the election, but he was quick to deny this. 'I showed the political restraint that befits a Civil Servant, and contented myself for the most part with addressing innumerable envelopes.' He had, however, taken a very close interest in the contest, both locally and nationally, and was disgusted by the spectacle. 'The Conservative candidate [Sir Richard Wells, a brewer], who had sat for the last 23 years, a nice, mild old man, had little to say on any subject except Private Enterprise (he did not go into details), and Mr Churchill. Asked whether he agreed with the views expressed in Beveridge's *Full Employment in a Free Society*, he displayed complete ignorance of the subject-matter. The organisation was appalling – boredom, apathy, and defeatism (even in the Agent himself) rampant.' It was hardly surprising that the Labour candidate – 'an able and unpleasant-looking Fabian, a protégé of Stafford Cripps' – captured the seat by 288 votes.

What Edward had seen at Bedford prompted these general reflections:

> Sir Richard Wells and his like must go and not come back. I must confess I think the defeat was well earned. If by 'Private Enterprise' you mean that each person should have opportunity to develop his talents, and to make his contribution to the society in which we live, then I quite agree, but would add two provisos: first, that his contribution will almost certainly have to fit into a larger framework. To talk as if we lived in an era of innumerable one-man businesses is just plain nonsense. 'Planning' is not Nazi-mindedness, it is both proper and inevitable. Professor Hayek purports to dispute this, but what he really opposes, I think, is not 'planning' but 'the master-planner' – as to which I thoroughly agree with him. Secondly, I cannot see why men of all parties should not reflect on how far 'Private

Enterprise' in its pre-war form really led to general prosperity. The answer is that it decidedly did not, and I suspect that Lord Keynes's *General Theory of Employment, Interest and Money*, whose general thesis has been worked out in greater detail by some Oxford economists, and pilfered by Beveridge, was a pretty true analysis of the economic situation as of 1936. Unfortunately, like all economic theories, Keynes's has been misunderstood and over-simplified, and the T.U.C. thinks of it as having a relevance to 1945 which it certainly hasn't got. But to return, I do think that these considerations show that 'Private Enterprise' is no rule of thumb, but a basic assumption which requires frequent qualifications, in order that the real aim of the state – prosperity at home and peace abroad – should be achieved. The broadcasts of that extremely able (and very Socialistic) man Sir John Anderson, and, I think, Eden, emphasised this point clearly. But the same can hardly be said of Winston's broadcasts! I should have thought it would be difficult to say whether his first broadcast was worse tactics, worse taste, or worse politics.

This passage foreshadows not only Edward's future but also that of the Conservative Party, at any rate for the next thirty years. The most striking and characteristic note in it is contempt for amateurish ignorance. Sir Richard Wells simply did not know his stuff; he and his like had to go. Though their private virtues might be acknowledged and appreciated, the unfitness of such people to sit in the post-war House of Commons was, in Edward's view, manifest. Despite his own privileged background, he was an apostle of the new meritocratic Toryism.

He also felt, in 1945, that the Conservative Party had to accept the need for some economic planning in the overall national interest. Though he was eager enough to do battle with socialism when it took the form of a dogma and a panacea, he was unwilling to do so in the name of unqualified private enterprise. 'Socialism' was not invariably used by him as a dirty word (see his reference to Sir John Anderson), and his belief in the Invisible Hand was never absolute. It seemed to him that the best way to fight the doctrinaire excesses of the Left was not to be equally doctrinaire in the opposite sense, but to be unashamedly moderate and pragmatic.

At the end of 1945 we met again at Oxford and I was surprised by two changes in him. Physically, he had lost a lot of weight and seemed almost gaunt compared with what he used to be. Metaphysically, he had abandoned his irreverent agnosticism and become a High Anglican. Neither of these changes was to prove permanent.

While we were at Oxford I saw less of him than at Eton or subsequently. We were in different colleges and moved in rather different grooves. Above all, he was extremely active in the Union and the University Conservative Association (OUCA), whereas I did not join the former and played little part in the latter. He was already preparing himself for a career in politics with all the dedication and professionalism whose absence he had so deplored in Sir Richard Wells.

In 1949, when we had both left Oxford, we became closely involved again as collaborators on the independent Conservative monthly, the *National Review* (later *National and English Review*), control of which had passed to my family from the Maxses. At first my father was the editor, with Edward and myself as assistants, and together the three of us would produce the long editorial feature, 'Episodes of the Month', which Leo Maxse and after him his sister, Lady Milner, had in their day made such a vehicle for militant partisanship. Every month we would travel down to pass the proofs at the Whitefriars Press at Tonbridge, breaking for lunch at the Rose and Crown. I think Edward enjoyed these expeditions. He and my father got on well, since they were both entirely free from generation-snobbery and recognised each other's very different strengths. The head printer with whom we used to deal, Mr Knowles, was sturdily honest in his opinions. One day, when he found us discussing Shakespeare, he told us exactly where he stood on the subject of the Bard. 'I know some people think a lot of him,' he said, 'but personally I've never had any time for him.' Edward was delighted by this comment, not because he shared the opinion but because he always appreciated genuine characters and views unaffected by conventional wisdom.

The *Review* may have looked rather old-fashioned, but it had interesting contributors and provided an outlet for some new writers with brilliant futures, such as John Bayley and Kenneth Rose, as well as for the younger generation of Conservatives, among whom Edward was outstanding. Much that he wrote was unsigned, in the 'Episodes of the Month', but he also wrote a fair number of signed pieces. These are of special value not only in themselves, but also because, sadly, he left so little in print. For anyone seeking to understand the quality of his mind and the nature of his Conservatism they are an indispensable source.

By no means all of them are political. They include pieces on the Three Choirs Festival, Sir Pelham Warner, England in the twelfth century, the early Tudors and the Chatham administration of 1766–68. But politics in one form or another is the commonest theme, with the treatment often strikingly uncommon. One of the very best is a long review article on Roy Harrod's life of Keynes, which appeared in the March 1951 issue. Dealing with *The Economic Consequences of the Peace*, Edward says he has no wish to defend the obtuseness of Hughes or Cunliffe, but believes all the same that

> Germany could have paid reparations on the scale which Keynes suggested, and that it was Keynes himself who must bear a large share of the responsibility for the fact that she did not do so, since the whole effect of the book was to convince the average Englishman that not only reparations, but the whole basis of the Versailles Treaty, were wrong in principle.

On Harrod's admission that Keynes gave insufficient attention to the problem of French security he comments: 'This is certainly an understatement.'

So much for Keynes's influence on British foreign policy. What of his influence at home? Though no amount of sophistry could justify the claim that he was a socialist, his name was nevertheless being invoked by many left-wing politicians. Was this his fault?

> Did Keynes fail to realise what would be the impact of his analysis on the thought of the Left? If so, then I fear he was guilty of an error of foresight as great as that which he committed in 1919. It may also be claimed . . . that Keynes in his later works aimed too high. If he had realised how far politicians have always to take into account the contingent and the unforeseen, he would have recognised that there could be no such thing as the 'general theory' of employment. I doubt if he ever realised the full sting of the remark by his brilliant pupil, F. P. Ramsey, that the most dangerous examples of inexact thinking arise from treating concepts that are necessarily vague as though they were precise. These reflections do not affect Keynes's right to a place among the very greatest of British economists. But they should make one pause before accepting his ideas too uncritically.

Nothing better illustrates Edward's professional approach to politics in the new age than the pains he took to master economics. By the time he became an MP in 1950 he could pass for an authority on the subject, though he had not read it at Oxford, and in the House of Commons he soon demonstrated that he could argue on equal terms with trained economists like Gaitskell, Wilson and Crosland. He showed the same self-confidence in print, as in a 'Reply to Mr Gaitskell' that appeared in the March 1952 issue of the *Review*:

> I really cannot take seriously Mr Gaitskell's suggestion that, if there have to be economies in consumption, it would have been better to impose a statutory limitation on dividends. This is just frivolous nonsense. The economies on the Health Service alone are calculated to save rather more than £20 million in a full year. On the other hand, the total increase in dividends for the years 1947–50 amounted altogether to some £3 million. It is absurd to suggest that the two figures are in any way comparable. Mr Gaitskell would no doubt wish to reply that the value of dividend limitation would be its likely effect on wage claims. Personally, I have never believed that dividend limitation would have any such effect, and in any case the other arguments against it are, in my view, overwhelming.

A year later he is arguing the case for reducing estate duty, on moral and social, no less than economic, grounds. Deploring the effect of the existing penal rates on small family businesses, he says it is quite clear 'there is no more powerful incentive towards the creation of new wealth than the desire of a man to leave his family better provided for.' People tried to evade the issue by pointing out that no-one could any longer earn a fortune, anyway; but 'this only proves that the level of direct taxation – especially on the higher ranges of earned income – is also too high.' His idea of the tolerable upper limits of taxation – three-quarters on income and three-fifths on an estate – may seem over-cautious by contemporary standards. But in 1953 it represented quite a challenge to the ruling fiscal orthodoxy.

It is a great pity that Edward did not write more during his life. He had so much to say, but said it all too seldom on paper. His style improved with practice, and of course would have improved still more if he had written more. It could be very pithy, as when he ended his review of a book on President Truman: 'He [Truman] has done his very best for the American people, according to his lights; and he was worthy of a better book than Mr Hillman has written.' But his pieces tended to suffer from the too frequent intrusion of phrases appropriate to the spoken word, such as 'in my opinion' or 'I should have thought', and there were moments of self-parody, such as the opening of an early article for the *Review* (in February 1949): 'As I sit at my desk, I well remember the first meeting of the Conservative Central Council that I ever attended. It was in the spring of 1946 . . . '

This habit of suggesting an almost endless background of thought and experience, already evident, as I have shown, in his teens, did not become less marked with the passage of time. Did it reflect a slight streak of pomposity in him? Not really – and in any case he had none of the serious faults of which pomposity may be a symptom. He was in no way a snob; he had an excellent sense of humour, which included being able to see himself in a funny light; and he was genuinely humble.

As a speaker he was most effective when debating.His style was not ideally suited to the public platform, since he preferred reasoned argument to ringing assertion. But he never talked down to audiences, and this helped him even on the stump, when he was not in his element. His character was appreciated, even if his words were not always understood. Once, when I was a candidate at Oldham and he had come up to help me, he was speaking to a small group of people at a street corner. As he explained the intricacies of tax policy and the balance of payments, a little old woman with a shopping bag, who had been standing in front of him muttering to herself, suddenly shouted, 'That's right, love, get the buggers out,' and hurried away. Everybody laughed, including Edward, and as a result the speech was more of a success than it might otherwise have been.

In 1954 he joined the government as a parliamentary secretary (for Supply). A day or two later my father met Churchill at a dinner of the Other Club and congratulated him on making the appointment. Churchill replied that he was somewhat reluctant to do it, because Edward was slightly younger than he (Churchill) had been when he first became a minister. But, he said, talents such as Edward's could not be denied; there was no choice but to appoint him.

For the previous three years Edward had been a PPS, but had nevertheless continued to play his part in editing the *Review*. As a minister he could no longer do this, but we kept in close touch. Only a year after his first appointment he was moved to the Treasury as Economic Secretary: notably swift promotion. At the Treasury he served, in turn, under the two men who were soon to be rival contenders for the premiership. He liked them both. Of R. A. Butler he used to say that he was in many ways a Victorian character – a description also, perhaps, applicable to himself. With Harold Macmillan he enjoyed discussing ideas. Both men were entertaining gossips.

In the ordinary course of events Edward could have expected to be a Cabinet minister well before the end of the decade. But the course of events was far from ordinary. In the autumn of 1956 the Eden government, faced with the admittedly provocative, but not in itself materially threatening, nationalisation of the Suez Canal Company by President Nasser, launched an attack on Egypt in alliance with the French and in secret collusion with Israel. During the weeks preceding the attack Britain's Commonwealth partners and American ally were systematically deceived as to the government's intentions. This disgraceful and calamitous act took most members of the government completely by surprise. For Edward the only premonition of it was a remark made to him by Macmillan at Birch Grove one day early in the crisis. They had been discussing Treasury matters but, as Edward was leaving, Suez was briefly mentioned on the doorstep, and in reply to what seemed a self-evident statement from Edward – that it would be unthinkable for us to go to war over the Canal Company – Macmillan said that he wondered if we could afford *not* to go to war. Edward more or less discounted the remark even at the time; and, since it was never repeated, put it out of his mind.

When the 'armed conflict' began he was, therefore, no less flabbergasted than I was. The ultimatum to Egypt and Israel was transparently phoney, its only conceivable object being to provide a pretext for invading Egypt. The analogy that Eden and others were drawing between Nasser and Hitler was ludicrous. Even if the nationalisation of the Company were to lead, at some stage, to the denial of freedom to use the Canal – which there was no reason whatever to assume it would – the resultant threat to Britain's vital interests would in no way compare with that posed by Hitler in the 1930s. Meanwhile the pre-emptive violence in which the government was engaged was sure to damage those very interests to an incalculable degree. Quite apart from the material cost, the loss of Britain's hard-won reputation for decency and maturity was agonising to contemplate.

From the very first Edward felt he had to resign. But there was nothing in his temperament, or in his understanding of politics, that encouraged him to take the step. On the contrary, he was a natural insider, to whom the role of rebel was profoundly uncongenial. Though always independent in his thinking, he liked to work with colleagues and to be part of a team. Moreover, he had no illusions as to the probable effect of resignation on his career. He had read too much history to have any confidence at all that resigning would be to his advantage, even if events were to vindicate his stand. He also knew that an act which would be perilous enough for a senior minister was bound to be far more so for a junior one, more especially when – as became apparent – no senior minister was prepared to resign with him. There was not a trace of bravado in Edward's resignation on the Suez issue. It was an act of pure political courage, for which he suffered in his career but which constitutes his chief claim, as a politician, to the admiration of posterity.

The shameful folly of Suez would not, he believed, have occurred if Churchill had been prime minister when Nasser nationalised the Canal Company. He recalled that in 1951, when Mossadek nationalised the Anglo-Iranian Oil Company and right-wing Conservatives were clamouring for force to be used against Iran, Churchill (then Leader of the Opposition) made a robustly moderate speech to the 1922 Committee, in which he argued that it would be demeaning for a great country like Britain to allow itself to be provoked into ill-considered action by a trivial and farcical figure like Mossadek. The trick worked, and the Conservative Party did not become committed to advocating war with Iran.

Edward had no doubt, therefore, that the change from Churchill to Eden was disastrous, as things turned out. Yet he had no vindictive feelings against Eden, whom he had earlier much respected. Though it seemed to him, with hindsight, that Eden might always have been unsuited to the premiership, he felt that Churchill had made him wait for it far too long, and had then bequeathed it to him in difficult circumstances. He sympathised with Eden's efforts to escape from Churchill's shadow, and deplored the way he was goaded by the 'Suez group' of Conservative MPs, of which Macmillan's son-in-law, Julian Amery, was one of the leaders.

During his short period out of office Edward returned to the *National and English Review*, in whose issue of January 1957 he replied to an article by Lord Attlee on the subject of party discipline. Attlee's contention was that party discipline must always be paramount (a line which explains his own pathetic votes against rearmament before the war). Edward's reply, entitled 'No, not quite . . . ', first cites as exceptions 'those questions which transcend party political boundaries – religion, capital punishment, divorce law reform, Sunday laws, betting laws, and so on.' But his further, more important, exception has a direct relevance to his own position:

> The other occasion on which, as it seems to me, a Member can rightly disagree with his local association occurs when he is honestly convinced that his party leaders have made a grave blunder on a major issue of crucial importance. I do not want to become too personal at this point, but it is perhaps worth remarking that no one has suggested that the Suez affair was not of sufficient *importance* to justify resignation from the Government; and for my part I simply cannot see how my own attitude, in deploring what was done, can be regarded as contrary to Conservative principles and beliefs. But it is at this point that Lord Attlee and I part company, because he would seem to regard my own failure to support the Government as in itself a breaking of bounds. 'If the Member [so Attlee had written] fails to support the Government, or fails to act with the Opposition in their efforts to turn the Government out, he is acting contrary to the expectation of those who have put their trust in him.' I can only repeat that I think one is entitled to take this action provided, first, that the issue is of sufficient importance and, secondly, that one's reasons for so acting do not run counter to the policy which one has previously put to the electors.

This might surely be accepted as the unwritten law – another Boyle's law – governing acts of individual rebellion within our political system.

Soon after that article appeared Edward was back in office. On 9 January 1957 Eden resigned, and through the inscrutable processes whereby Conservative leaders were then chosen Macmillan emerged as his successor. The new Prime Minister – whose conduct in the Suez affair had been singularly outrageous – was keen to have Edward in his government, partly because he had observed his talents at close quarters at the Treasury, and was fond of him, but above all because he wanted to give the government and party an appearance of unity under his leadership. At the same time he did not wish to suggest that Edward's resignation had been justified; if anything he wished to

convey the opposite impression. He therefore offered Edward a post
– that of junior minister for Education – significantly lower than the
one he had left, while offering Julian Amery the under-secretaryship
at the War Office. Both offers were accepted, with the result that
Edward was, in effect, punished for being right, while Julian was
rewarded for being wrong.

Throughout the Suez crisis Edward not only shared his thoughts
with me almost daily, but also consulted me. He did not consult me
about his decision to return to office on Macmillan's terms, though
he did telephone to give me the news before it was made public.
Had he asked my opinion I should have strongly advised him against
returning on such terms, and it was because he knew I would do this
that he did not ask me. It seemed to me then, and seems still, that
he should have assured Macmillan of his general support for the
new government, and of his willingness to serve in it provided he
could do so without appearing in any way to weaken or derogate
from the stand he had taken when he resigned. In other words, he
should have insisted at the very least upon returning to his old post
at the Treasury, if not upon being given a more important post. To
accept demotion was, surely, a mistake.

It was two years before he regained the rank he had held at the
time of his resignation, and five years before he was admitted to the
Cabinet, when the long period of Conservative rule that began in
1951 was nearing its end. As a Cabinet minister he was exclusively
concerned with education, and when the party was in opposition
after 1964 he was stuck with the same subject for much of the time,
only leaving it to deal with that of home affairs. Both were difficult
subjects for a man of his rational, tolerant, undoctrinaire outlook to
handle in the increasingly ideological climate of Conservative politics
in the late 1960s. When he reluctantly came to the conclusion that
he would not be given more congenial work to do as a Tory
front-bencher, he accepted the Vice-Chancellorship of Leeds – and
was then stuck with education for the rest of his life.

Of course he contributed much to the educational world, and
gained much from it. All the same, it was a grave misfortune
that his unique qualities were lost to the State for the last decade
of his life. He was not 'wet' or 'dry' as those terms have lately
been used, but a Tory with a formidable combination of intellect,
character and conscience, who was denied the opportunity to prove
his full worth.

5

Cricket and Race Relations

David Lane

I first knew Edward Boyle at Eton in the late 1930s and early 1940s. He went there just after his 13th birthday, a boy of outstanding talent. I was a year older, and we were never in the same form either during our early years or as seniors when he specialised in History and I in Classics. His academic achievements were conspicuous, however, and he and his close friend John Grigg were also recognised and admired by the rest of us for their knowledge of current affairs and their debating flair. All this, plus music and cricket and other interests, made Boyle a quite exceptional schoolboy.

It was mainly at cricket that our paths crossed in those days. With his physique Boyle could never be a star performer at outdoor sports. But he loved cricket and was an expert observer of the game, and he applied his mind to the art of scoring. In 1941 he became scorer for the First XI. That was a strange summer – for some of us the last before war service. With Britain standing alone, Hitler turning from his conquest of continental Europe to attack Russia, Crete lost and the fortunes of war see-sawing in the Western Desert, inter-school cricket in England continued as keenly as ever (apart from one day a week when we dug for victory). Boyle was meticulous in recording all the details of our contests, and I like to think that his expertise helped to uplift our performance on the field. In later life he would surely have scored for England if he had not devoted his energies to even more important things.

The captain of the Eton XI in 1942, Edwin Bramall (now Field Marshal Lord Bramall) has these recollections of Scorer Boyle:

> He had an abiding interest in and knowledge of cricket, almost as deep as his love of church music. He knew Wisden backwards and had a photographic memory about match results and individuals' performances, scores and averages. He was a brilliant scorer keeping, as well as an immaculate score book, individual charts for each batsman to show how he had made his runs and to which

part of the field his scoring shots had gone. This was invaluable to the batsman in trying to improve his game for the future.

As Captain in 1942, I also found him an invaluable tactical adviser. Being a highly modest and diffident man (although with a steel core underneath) he never forced his views on anyone, but he was a wonderful sounding board for a captain's ideas and his advice, if asked for, was always given with the greatest honesty and integrity.

In fact he made such a contribution to cricket in that year, which was a very successful year for the First XI, that I gave him his 'Strawberry Mess' [roughly equivalent to Third XI Colours]. This was very well received.

The great thing about Edward is that, although he was so wise and indeed so much cleverer than all of us, he was so human and humble about it and never made one feel less intellectual than him. He, in his turn, liked to feel part of the team. He was a great believer in the bridge between the intellectual and the athletic to make up the complete life, and he enjoyed his contacts with games players (non-intellectuals if you like) very much indeed.

Boyle's love of cricket endured. He enjoyed going to the Parks at Oxford and, as an MCC member, to Lord's. He was a keen follower of Sussex, and Mr E. W. Swanton remembers several meetings with him and his mother as spectators at Hove. Later, in Yorkshire, when his busy schedule as Vice-Chancellor of Leeds University allowed, he went to Headingley to see a Test Match or a county game.

After school our paths did not cross again for over twenty years. During the 1950s and early 1960s I watched with admiration Boyle's entry into politics and rapid advance in the Conservative ranks. Elected Member of Parliament for Handsworth in 1950, he soon became a junior minister. His resignation from the government over the Suez adventure, which he deplored, was an act of real courage at a time when passions were running high in the Conservative Party and in the country as a whole. His readiness to take such a stand on a matter of major policy, regardless of personal consequences, made a strong impression on me and on many others at that troubled time. Before long, however, he was invited by Mr Macmillan to rejoin the government.

Although concerned with national affairs through most of his years in the House of Commons, Boyle was an assiduous constituency member. No one could describe Handsworth, part of the

Birmingham inner-city, as a typical Conservative seat. Few Tories, I believe, could have held it throughout the 1960s, when the pendulum had swung against the party. Boyle's success in doing so, despite the unhappiness of some of his constituency workers over his views on controversial issues, was a testimony to his wide appeal among uncommitted voters.

Handsworth was one of the first constituencies to experience an inflow of Commonwealth immigrants different in colour and culture from the majority of the population. Boyle had an eye for major issues, and he straightaway saw race relations as a matter of principle and of supreme importance for Britain's future. Being an ardent one-nation Conservative he recognised the new threat to this ideal in the late twentieth century if racial discrimination was not confronted and stamped out. As early as November 1967, in the first Carr-Saunders memorial lecture, Boyle with his wide view of the national scene was drawing attention to the special educational needs of immigrant children. Commenting on a survey of performance at a school in southwest London, he said:

> This is a very important result. It shows that racial discrimination and a willingness to treat minority groups as second-class citizens is not only morally intolerable but also hopelessly wasteful of potential talent.

He then spelled out five priorities, which have remained prominent ever since in the debate on multicultural education in Britain. About race relations generally, he remarked in the same lecture:

> It does seem to me enormously important that politicians should be not only humanitarian but also as clear-headed and sure-footed as possible in their approach to this subject. In the first place we have to ensure that immigrants, and especially coloured immigrants, are not made the scapegoat for problems that, as a community, we have failed to solve.

Also during the 1960s he joined with others outside Parliament in taking initiatives designed to improve race relations, including the foundation of the Runnymede Trust. Inside Parliament he was one of a number of like-minded Tories striving to counter the racialist tendencies in the party that had surfaced during the Smethwick election campaign.

Boyle, although relatively young, was already a senior and influential Conservative and shadow Minister of Education when I entered the House of Commons late in 1967. He went out of his way to make me welcome. It was a difficult time for the party. Being in opposition in the Commons is always frustrating. In addition there were deep divisions of view among Conservatives on two topical issues, race relations and education, both of which were of great concern to Boyle. Those of us on the liberal wing of the party took heart from his courageous public stance on such issues. We were not a tightly organised group and we had no clandestine link with him, but in our own discussions and activities as back-benchers we knew that his voice would always be raised in the Shadow Cabinet on the side of reason and humanity.

Early in 1968 the Labour Government published its Race Relations Bill, in order to make more effective the counter-measures against racial discrimination. Before Second Reading the Shadow Cabinet put down a reasoned amendment declining to support the Bill on various grounds. Two days later, on the eve of the Second Reading debate, Mr Powell made his inflammatory 'rivers of blood' speech and Mr Heath (to his eternal credit) dismissed him from the Shadow Cabinet. At the end of the debate Boyle and several of us on the back benches abstained from voting for the Shadow Cabinet's amendment, which we thought was a wrong response to the Bill. It was almost unprecedented for a member of the Shadow Cabinet to abstain in such a vote, and Boyle's action – again illustrating his courage in sticking to his convictions at whatever risk to his career – caused a major furore. Part of his statement of explanation read:

> I abstained because I felt that I could not, on conscientious grounds, oppose the second reading of the Race Relations Bill.
>
> This Bill, whatever its imperfections, will surely do two things.
>
> First, it will make it clear that Britain is determined to secure equal rights for all its citizens. Second, it will provide a means whereby racial discrimination over a wide area can be checked. The PEP and Street reports convince me, as they have convinced many other people, both of the extent to which discrimination has already become common, and of the impact which law can have in the field of race relations.
>
> I believe this is a subject of major importance and that we must break out of what has been described as the vicious circle in which a black face means a poor job, a home in a bad neighbourhood,

and therefore a school below average standard for the children.

Mr Heath's decision to keep him in the Shadow Cabinet was also controversial. The respect for Boyle in the parliamentary party, most of whom did not wholly share his views on race relations, was shown by the overwhelming defeat of a campaign led by Sir Gerald Nabarro to force Mr Heath to change his mind and sack his 'rebel' colleague. Boyle's action at that time, I am sure, helped to persuade the party not to oppose the Bill on its eventual third reading. In consequence, and greatly to the national benefit, there has been a broad area of inter-party consensus on race relations during the succeeding years.

In March 1969 Boyle showed once more his clear vision and political courage on this issue. Speaking at Reading University he suggested that Mr Powell was encouraging Britain to talk itself into a quite unnecessary race relations crisis. Two equal and opposite mistakes, Boyle argued, were possible – to assume that there was no problem or to talk ourselves into a crisis by indulging in prophecies of inevitable doom. The second had become the greater danger, 'due in considerable measure to the baleful genius of one politician who has made himself, whether we like it or not, a household name.'

Boyle went on to appeal to the traditional British causes of tolerance, justice, fair dealing and social concern. There must be no harassment, no suggestion that, with a policy of sour looks and repatriation grants, Britain could eliminate the problems of living together. Strict control of new immigrant numbers must continue, but it was just as important to recognise the real benefits of cultural diversity, and the part coloured labour was playing in the growth industries and essential services.

In 1970 Boyle spoke out freely against the projected South African cricket tour to England (which was eventually cancelled). On 14 May the House of Commons discussed the issue in a highly-charged debate. Boyle – making what turned out to be his last speech in the Commons, because Parliament was dissolved two weeks later – explained why he had agreed to become a vice-chairman of the Fair Cricket Campaign:

> I did so because, as someone who utterly deplores and opposes violence and disorder, I had come reluctantly to the view that the South African cricket tour was likely to be bad for community relations in this country, bad for the future of cricket, bad for

the future of sport generally, bad for the Commonwealth, and bad for law and order in Britain. . . .

I have always believed that the links of sport, and not least those of cricket, were among the most valuable links binding the Commonwealth together. I remember an occasion when Mr Harold Macmillan, as Prime Minister, was going to the West Indies. At the time, I was a junior minister at the Treasury. A message came to my private office asking if, then and there, I could draft a passage on West Indian cricket for inclusion in one of Mr Macmillan's speeches. I can recall the enthusiasm with which I wrote of some of the achievements of the three Ws – Weekes, Walcott and Worrell.

It is precisely those of us who value most the links which I have mentioned, who question most earnestly the wisdom of going ahead with the South African tour this summer.

The second issue causing serious conflicts of view within the party in those years was education, Boyle's own responsibility in the Shadow Cabinet. The Labour government was accelerating the switch to a comprehensive system. Many Conservatives were passionately opposed to this; others, including local councillors with long practical experience, acknowledged the weaknesses in the existing system and the strength of parts of the pro-comprehensive case. The former of the two factions was more vocal. Each autumn, often in the face of ugly barracking, Boyle bravely went through the ordeal of replying to the education debate at the Party Conference and sticking to the reasoned, pragmatic policy which he and the Shadow Cabinet favoured; and he invariably won the argument.

In October 1969 it was announced that Boyle was to be appointed Vice-Chancellor of Leeds University and would be leaving the Shadow Cabinet and (soon) the House of Commons. I remember the consternation with which one or two of us read the news as we paused at the tape machine near the Members' dining room. Instinctively we felt it as a very severe blow. We could not persuade him to change his mind, and we had to respect his reasons: the certain opportunity of playing a leading, full-time role in the development of education in Britain appealed to him even more than the prospects, as he saw them, of continuing involvement in politics.

The sense of loss was also expressed in newspapers such as *The Times*. In a leading article it praised Boyle as one of those

> who exert a political influence beyond their personal achievements or capacities. . . . His departure from the Tory front bench is a loss to his party and to British politics in general not so much because of his administrative talents, considerable though these are, but because he has become the liberal conscience of the Tory party. There are men on the Opposition front bench of greater political stature, but nobody whose public position on a range of issues is such a faithful reflection of genuinely liberal responses.

It went on to recall three questions on which Boyle's 'independent spirit has been especially valuable' – Suez, race relations and comprehensive schools; and commented:

> This preserving of the balance over a range of issues has been his special contribution to the Tory party, particularly during these years in opposition. Humane and compassionate, informed by a knowledge of what is actually happening in society, he is in what might be termed the Butler tradition of the party.

For many practising and would-be politicians of the 1950s and 1960s Boyle set an inspiring example. His admirers will always remember his large physical presence, his vision and intellect, and above all (borrowing Dr Martin Luther King's phrase) the content of his character. He was an influence for good inside and outside Parliament, not least among students. There were times when Boyle's prominent position in the party, more than anything else, persuaded wavering citizens to continue to put their trust in the Conservatives.

He had not the gift of moving a mass audience by high-flown oratory, but he brought into politics something no less valuable and all too rare – great brain-power coupled with sympathetic understanding. He focussed unerringly on the big issues and never hesitated to back unpopular causes if he thought them right. He was not one for cheap applause or for the easy option of swimming with an emotional tide or adopting facile solutions. With his moral courage he preferred the harder way of honesty, integrity and rational argument. He was a man of sensitivity, civilised and tolerant. All these and other qualities shone out. Since 1970 British politics have been the poorer for his absence.

But Boyle would have been ill-at-ease, I suspect, in the adversarial, polarised politics of today. So far as the Conservative Party is concerned he would probably have applauded much that has been achieved by Mrs Thatcher's government but disliked the less attractive features of Conservatism in the 1980s. Narrowness of mind and hardness of face, over-emphasis on individualism, ideology pushed to extremes, simplistic thinking, the arrogant tendency – these Conservative aberrations would have worried him very much. Fair and broad in outlook and rigorous in thought, he favoured a more balanced approach to national issues. Both party and country would benefit from a greater infusion of the Boyle philosophy in the politics and politicians of the 1990s.

6

The Oxford Union and After
Tony Benn

Edward was a contemporary at Oxford just after the war, and it was then that I first met him. He was at Christ Church, and everyone who came across him was at once impressed by his scholarly and benign nature and by the fact that he talked to everybody in exactly the same way, making no distinction between them. Thus despite his obvious ability he never created any barrier between himself and others, save only that his manner was already that of a middle-aged man, and his appearance that of some college don cast improbably amongst the students. His interests were very academic and he would speak of them without any awareness of the response that his remarks might produce on his hearers, which meant that no-one ever felt put down by him, even if they did not really understand what he was saying, for the kindliness of his demeanour flattered rather than insulted their intelligence.

In politics he was earnest and fair-minded, a Tory of the old-fashioned kind whose inspiration seemed to be essentially paternalist, being motivated both by the demands of logic and a genuine concern for the well-being of humanity at large – in the manner of the Liberal Government of 1906 in which the early Churchill served.

His speeches at the Oxford Union which won him election to the offices of that club were always serious and listened to with the respect which they deserved, and it was through our common membership of the Union that he and Kenneth Harris and I were selected to go to America for the first post-war debating tour in the winter of 1947–48 – a five-month trip that took us to 60 universities and colleges in 42 states. For all of us, coming from the austerities of post-war Britain, this tour created an immensely strong impression and Kenneth Harris's book *Travelling Tongues* caught the spirit of it most excellently.

Edward found America and American ways strange in the extreme, and some of the things that happened to us – and to him – gave rise to great hilarity. On the very first day there, when we had been put up in the Harvard Club in New York City, we were introduced to the buffet lunch which I suspect Edward found very unfamiliar. He was not a very practical person and when he saw the coffee urn being used he wrongly deduced that it was a pump, which had to be moved backwards and forwards to produce results. This he did, as little spurts of coffee fell into his cup, causing much merriment to those who were waiting, but unfortunately, having filled it to the brim he left the tap in the middle – or ON – position so that as he moved on, a powerful jet of boiling coffee continued to pour on to the carpet.

In his speeches to American student audiences Edward was as impressive as he had been at home, and his mature look, manner and learning were most effective in showing up the more formalistic forensic skills which were then being taught in a rather mechanistic way to the students of Debates.

Edward had a great sense of humour and I can recall many occasions when he burst out in a fit of laughter that seemed to shake his entire frame and was highly infectious. He could also be very critical of American civilisation and on one occasion, in Arizona, where it was very hot, Edward stood, in the bathroom, in his long woolly underwear which he had brought from home, drinking whisky out of a bakelite tooth mug and describing Abraham Lincoln's Gettysburg address as 'a load of rubbish'.

I recall that he was deeply shocked when he discovered, while we were staying at the British Embassy in Washington, that his wallet had been stolen in a drive-in café which we had visited. He persuaded the British Ambassador to lend him the official Rolls-Royce to go back and look for it, only to learn that the wallet itself had been dumped in a trash bin, the dollars gone but the pounds sterling left as worthless.

We were both elected to Parliament within a few weeks of each other and it was not long before Edward had made his mark on the House, and on his colleagues in the Conservative Party, so that it came as no surprise to anyone when he was appointed to ministerial office, a responsibility he discharged with dignity and effectiveness. It was during his period on the government front bench that the troubling of his conscience began to play a part in the development of his own later life, for he was committed to causes that, even then, made him suspect amongst some of the right-wing of his own party, as for example when he voted, on a free vote, for the abolition of the death penalty. The real test came

1. Edward Boyle, aged 7, with his mother, his brother and sister and their nanny.

2. (*above*) Aged 12, on a sightseeing visit to Hamburg with his father.

3. (*below*) At Oxford in 1947, with fellow-officers at the University Conservative Association. On his left Margaret Roberts, later Mrs. Thatcher.

4. (*above*) In 1948 as President of the Oxford Union with his guest speaker, Lord Balfour of Inchyre.

5. (*below*) At a garden party in his constituency in the early 1950s.

6. As Minister of Education.

7. Sir Alec Douglas-Home's cabinet in July 1964. Left to right (*seated*) Selwyn Lloyd, Edward Heath, Henry Brook, Lord Dilhorne, R. A. Butler Sir Alec Douglas-Home, Quintin Hogg, Reginald Maudling, Duncan Sandys, Peter Thorneycroft, Lord Blakenham. Edward Boyle, Minister of Education and Science, standing behind Reginald Maudling.

8. Taking his seat in the House of Lords in 1970, with his supporters, Lord Butler of Saffron Walden and Lord Fulton of Falmer.

9. As Chairman of the 1972 Jury of the Leeds Band Competition talking to Mlle. Nadia Boulanger.

10. With the prize-winners of the 1972 Leeds Piano Competition (*left to right*) Eugene Indjk, Murray Perahia and Craig Sheppard.

11. (*above*) Conferring an Honorary Degree on Mlle. Nadia Boulanger in 1972.

12. (*below*) As Vice-Chancellor of Leeds University with Chancellor H.R.H. The Duchess of Kent, the Pro-Chancellor Sir Richard Graham and the Honorary Graduates of 1973.

with Suez, to which he was personally opposed and for the very best of reasons, when he resigned his position and returned to the back benches.

He returned to office in the Ministry of Education and later became the Minister: that must surely have been the happiest time in his political life for it was a subject in which he had a deep interest and since that government, under Harold Macmillan and in which Rab Butler also served, was very sympathetic to what Edward wanted to do, so he must have felt that he was swimming with the political tide.

I must record his very great personal kindnesses to me over all these years, especially during my own constitutional struggles to escape from the House of Lords, when Edward was always ready with advice, encouragement and above all inside information which greatly assisted me in planning a strategy that would allow me to defeat the Cabinet of which he was a member, all done without the slightest hint of disloyalty, on his part, to his colleagues. Indeed, in the by-election in Bristol in April 1961 when I was standing as a disqualified candidate, after the House had expelled me on grounds of my peerage, Edward, who had been sent to speak on the Conservative platform, then came over to meet my supporters in a local hotel and expressed his own personal backing, as he later did financially, when an appeal was launched to pay my legal costs in the court case which followed.

I was privileged to meet his mother to whom he was devoted, his sister and his brother, and spent a night at their house when he asked me to come and speak at some local function on a non-political subject, and no account of his life would be complete without a recognition of the role which family loyalty played in his own mind and make-up.

The last time I met him was when he was, characteristically, undertaking his final act of public service, as chairman of the Boyle Committee which was charged with the task of fixing higher salaries that could not be negotiated in the normal way. I had to make the case for the chairman of the British National Oil Corporation which, as Secretary of State, I had just established, and he cross-examined me closely and courteously, and then, later, declared the result of his adjudication.

Edward's knowledge and love of music played a large role in his life and, though I am in no way qualified to assess his talents in that direction, music was his great interest, and must have given him solace and pleasure of a kind not so easily obtained in the hurly-burly of an active political life.

His early death deprived British public life of a kindly and distinguished public servant, and deprived his many friends and admirers of a good and honest friend, but the many warm memories of this charming and talented man remain as bright today as they ever did during his lifetime.

7
At the Treasury
Robert Neild

My first meeting with Edward after childhood was at the Treasury in the office of the Chancellor of the Exchequer, Rab Butler, just after he had presented his autumn budget in 1955. It was a meeting which led to a rapport between Edward and me – a rapport in which economic policy and the way it was formed in government were our main ground of common interest. To explain how that happened, it is necessary to stand back and tell a tale.

I had had a hand in making the economic forecast for the Budget in April in which income tax was reduced shortly before an election. The economic forecast had suggested that the economy was running full and that a tax cut was not appropriate, but somehow the Chancellor had decided to take a risk and make a tax cut by reference to incentives. I was indignant about this. I remember going to Robert Hall, the head of the Economic Section, and saying, rather priggishly, that I hoped he had put it on record that the Economic Section advised against any tax cut.

During the summer the usual signs of an overheated economy – a balance of payments deficit and inflation – had shown themselves and credit had been tightened. In the autumn, when the financial markets and the financial side of the Treasury began to be alarmed, we had produced a new economic analysis saying that the budget needed to be tightened. Sir Edward Bridges, then the head of the Treasury and the Civil Service, had taken command and a budget package had swiftly been assembled. It provided for increases in indirect taxation, including the extension of purchase tax to some new items, including pots and pans. Some wag called it 'the pots and pans budget'.

The budget received a pretty bad reception. The next day I was instructed to attend a meeting in the Chancellor's office, something I had not done before. The Economic Section had been run down so far at that time – there were only about a dozen economists in the whole of government – that although I held a rank equivalent to a principal, it fell to me to stand in for Robert Hall.

The meeting, to advise on how best to defend the budget, was attended by Sir Edward Bridges and by a daunting array of knights and senior officials from the Treasury, the Revenue Departments and the Bank of England. But amongst them was Edward Boyle who a few months before had become Economic Secretary. I had not seen him since we had been at school together at Abinger Hill. When I was a nervous new boy there in the summer of 1935, he had been head of my dormitory, and I had liked him. Though older, he was benign, not at all authoritarian.

After we had all sat down at the conference table, the Chancellor sat for a minute or two at his desk in the far corner of the room, signing papers which his private secretary put before him. He looked uncomfortable. The arm which he had injured in childhood was curved forwards and he signed with his hand facing backwards. He got up and, having walked slowly to the table, stood at the end and, in his curiously plaintive voice, recounted how in the spring he had reduced the income tax to give the nation a fresh incentive; now he had raised taxation again to stop overheating. He ended, 'I am right, aren't I?' Swiftly, Bridges cried, 'Yes, Chancellor,' and his words were echoed by a chorus of the other great men round the table. I remained silent. I suppose Edward did so too.

After the meeting Edward asked me to go to his office. When we were alone together he asked, cautiously, whether he was correct in thinking that I did not believe the government had been right to lower the income tax in April. When I concurred, he replied, 'Thank goodness, that's the first bit of sense I have heard since I arrived here. I really cannot understand this place.' He opened up, questioning me closely about the economics of the spring and autumn budgets. After that we talked often about current economic policy, about economics and about the Treasury.

In the following days Edward was absorbed in defending the budget in the House of Commons. The Opposition attack was led, powerfully, by Hugh Gaitskell, the Shadow Chancellor.

The *Hansard* of those debates provides a reminder of how learned, civilised and good humoured was Edward, compared with politicians of today, and how effective he was in debate.

Turning to Hugh Gaitskell in a winding up speech he remarked,

I hope that the Right Hon. Member for Leeds, South, will understand that it is no discourtesy on our part if we sometimes accept his air of somewhat schoolmasterly infallibility with a slight pinch of salt.

When a Member suggested that evasion of hire purchase regulations was a problem, Edward replied,

If my hon. Friend the Member for Yeovil [Mr Peyton] will study certain statistics, which I will gladly send to him, he will see no reason to think that hire purchase restrictions are being widely evaded. [House of Commons Monthly Report, 28 October 1955, Col. 620.]

Mr Peyton replied – what else could he say – 'I am very much obliged to my hon. Friend.'

His Gladstonian quality comes out when he replies to a speech by Mr Grimond.

The hon. Gentleman also made some very interesting remarks about inflation, and suggested that we needed some new kind of enquiry. My view is that it would be a mistake to think that inflation is, as it were, purely a monetary phenomenon. It is a very complicated thing. [*Laughter*] I say this in all seriousness to the House. One of the valuable lessons which some modern philosophers have taught us is that problems which in the past have been thought to be largely unitary problems are in fact a complexus of interrelated problems. I think that exactly the same may very well be true about inflation. [HC Monthly Report, 8 November 1955, Col. 1791.]

Those debates on the autumn budget were tough going. A wounded Chancellor was being hounded by the Opposition. They attacked the government for political budgeting and they attacked the package of tax-raising measures that had been hastily assembled. Edward was particularly attacked for putting the paradoxical proposition that an increase in purchase tax, which raised prices, reduced inflation by taking demand out of the economy. It was called 'Boyle's Law'. But Edward stood his ground.

Edward, who liked and admired Rab Butler, supported him without stint. He felt concerned for Rab, whose wife was mortally ill and who seemed, as the debates went on, to be abandoned as a lame duck Chancellor.

Once the budget was out of the way, life calmed down. Edward reached out to the few of us who were still there as economic advisers in the Economic Section. He used to consult us individually in his office or over a good meal; and then I remember that for a time he held regular little seminars with us. The new Chancellor, Harold Macmillan, like Edward, was often dissatisfied with the kind of advice he got from the Treasury Old Guard. Edward seemed judiciously to be offering other views.

Edward approached economics with a strong concern for the social and moral assumptions on which any proposition rested and a concern for its relevance to policy. He had read widely. Politically, he belonged in that middle ground, which was then so wide, containing people who believed in market forces provided they were restrained when they did not lead to the public well-being. He was impatient of Hayek and Robbins with their seemingly unqualified admiration for market forces and their faith in running the economy by controlling the money supply and little else. He admired the works of Keynes, Dennis Robertson and Hubert Henderson, and he followed the works of Balogh and Kaldor quite closely. He would say of Tommy Balogh's attacks on free trade and free capital movements, 'I do think he has a point and cannot be dismissed out of hand.' He was much impressed by the richness of Nicky Kaldor's arguments, and by the concern for social justice which he displayed in his many articles on taxation. At the same time he rather mistrusted Nicky's readiness to produce a tax gadget to solve any problem.

Edward was one of those rare ministers – Tony Crosland was another – whom it was a pleasure to advise because they were interested in understanding the intellectual substance of the argument you offered; they did not impatiently scan the argument for a usable political tactic and then lose interest. Edward liked to hear the whole argument, to dig out the assumptions that lay beneath it, and think about the effects of the possible policies that might follow from it. He never seemed to be in a hurry; he liked to fit a new proposition into the great structure of knowledge which he carried around in his capacious mind. There was something of a learned Victorian bishop about him.

My next clear memories of Edward are over the Suez crisis. In the summer of 1956 an air of conspiracy could be felt in Whitehall. The circulation of Cabinet Minutes had been cut down. Meetings on economic affairs were less frequent than usual. Normal business seemed only to be ticking over. In the newspapers there were rumours of preparations for war. There was an exodus from the Treasury as senior officials, uncomfortable at what was going on and unable to do anything about it, went on holiday. Just before they left, two of us from the Economic Section – Fred Atkinson and I – were instructed to prepare an appraisal of the economic effects of anything that might happen at Suez. It was the last job I did before leaving to go on holiday and then take up a post at Cambridge. In doing it, I learnt a little about what was being planned. I used to compare notes with Edward, who learnt bits and pieces on the political grapevine. We were both very unhappy about the preparations for war.

The Suez War occurred soon after I had arrived in Cambridge that autumn. I read that Edward had resigned. Not long afterwards, he invited me to go and spend a weekend at his home in Sussex, where he lived with his mother. It was a formal household. You dressed for dinner and your clothes were unpacked and laid out by a manservant. There were no other guests. There was plenty of time to talk.

Edward, who was then on the back benches, told me about his resignation. He felt no doubts about what he had done, but he had had a difficult time with some of his party, which still troubled him and perhaps permanently diminished his appetite for politics. He had had to face his constituency party in Birmingham, and it had been a close run thing whether they would get rid of him. What really upset him was that afterwards the Chairman or Secretary of the local party – I forget which – with whom he was discussing what had happened at the meeting, said to him in a reflective mood, 'You know, Edward, it wouldn't have been so bad if you hadn't been against hanging too.' Recounting this, Edward, in a characteristic gesture, shook his arms up and down as if he was banging a table with both fists, and said, 'It really is very difficult sometimes to serve in a party which has people in it who think like that.'

I asked him whether he had thought of crossing the floor. He replied that he could not do that, he would not 'fit' the Labour Party. He was right, and I felt rather foolish for having raised the idea when I thought about it afterwards – though not at the time, for Edward never made you feel foolish.

After that I did not see much of Edward until the mid-1960s when we served together on the Fulton Committee on the reform of the Civil Service. Partly because of our experiences of the Civil Service in the 1950s, we held the same views about the need for the recruitment of people trained in subjects relevant to what they were going to do, in particular economics, the need for movement in and out of the Civil Service and for more scope for ministers to have their own advisers. Edward did not make the running very much. There were others to do that. His was the detached, reasonable voice of someone who knew that the reform of the Civil Service was not a partisan issue: both parties needed a more expert and flexible system. He would not chase the wilder hares that were let loose in the Committee, but he supported any reasonable reform. And he would not let the Civil Service in their evidence get away with the recitation of the conventional wisdom in defence of the existing system. Quietly but firmly, he helped the committee along.

I was then away in Sweden for nearly five years. After I returned I saw Edward from time to time. Then I heard that he was ill. I wrote to him, but I saw him no more.

If I try to visualise Edward, I see him most vividly at Abinger Hill, a boy whose good nature and prematurely wise view of the world seemed to make him invulnerable to the teasing which he might easily have suffered for being so large and fat – for regularly coming last in the obstacle race. He often seemed to be absorbed in thought, perhaps reciting to himself. He was gentle. He had no appetite for attack upon others. And he semeed extraordinarily learned even then.

When I met him again at the Treasury, he had not changed. He was just the same person, except that he seemed to have developed a philosophical, Christian strength.

8

In the House of Commons
Robert Rhodes James

I first 'met' Edward Boyle as an undergraduate, through the medium of *Any Questions* in the early 1950s. Television was a rarity, interest in politics was intense, and this, the most successful of all radio programmes, with a weekly audience of 16 million, first introduced me not only to Edward but to Hugh Gaitskell, Tony Benn, Quintin Hailsham, Bob Boothby and Michael Foot, all of whom subsequently became close personal friends, and several of them parliamentary colleagues.

Although I was, and always had been, fascinated by politics, I was not a partisan, and Oxford between 1952 and 1955 was notably apolitical. I did not join the Union or any Conservative club. I espied Michael Heseltine, Bryan Magee, Tim Rathbone, Malcolm Fraser and Julian Critchley from a distance. Our Member of Parliament was widely perceived, and rightly, as a disaster, and came to a sticky and ignominious end; in the 1955 General Election I cast my first vote for the Liberal candidate in North Dorset, where my family then lived. This, I suppose, was an admirable background for a junior clerk of the House of Commons, to which post I was appointed in 1955 when I left university, although my tutor, a wise and perceptive man, had written me down (or, given his then politics, off) as basically a Conservative – a fact of which I was unaware.

On one memorable occasion on *Any Questions*, of which I was a devotee because, unlike now, the members of the panel actually said what they meant and knew what they were talking about, Edward was asked for some memories of his schooldays, and spoke about Eton. The Labour MP sourly retorted that he and his class did not enjoy the same privileges, to which Edward heatedly replied that 'I was asked for my memories of my schooldays. I am not ashamed to have been at Eton,' upon which he received an immense and prolonged ovation from the audience. This is my first memory of him, and I thought I would like to know him better.

By the time I reached the Commons as a very young Clerk in 1955 Edward was already a legendary figure. He had been elected in 1950 at the absurdly early age of 27 and was already not only a minister but a very special one.

Parliamentary under-secretaries are the lowest form of ministerial life, and are made to feel it. The opportunities to shine are virtually non-existent, and those to return to oblivion are manifold. The first rung on the ladder is too often the last.

One afternoon in 1954 the then Minister of Supply was unable to attend the Commons for Questions, so Edward, as Parliamentary Under-Secretary, had to take over, and answer for the entire hour. Alas, I was not there, but in that hour a star was born. He held the House enraptured, and at the end, blushing scarlet, left the Chamber to an unparalleled ovation from both sides. Rarely has a junior minister received such a press as Edward did the following morning, and Edward Fellowes, my boss as Clerk of the House, who had been there since 1919 and seen everything, told me that it was the most amazing sustained personal *tour de force* he had ever witnessed in the House of Commons.

Edward's Parliamentary style was unique. It had a certain bubbling Billy Bunter quality of almost the eternal happy schoolboy, combined with a thoughtfulness and courtesy which always ensured him a very fair and respectful hearing. When he felt deeply on a subject he would redden, and although never losing his temper, his strength of feeling would become very manifest. It was a relaxed style, with much humour, and always pleased, interested ,and amused, the House of Commons.

When Eden became Prime Minister he appointed Edward Economic Secretary to the Treasury under Rab Butler, and we all spoke about an almost certain Prime Minister. This was confirmed during the stormy passage of what became known as Rab's 'pots and pans' Autumn Budget of 1955. It ended Rab's tenure at the Treasury, made Hugh Gaitskell leader of the Labour Party, and finished Herbert Morrison, but Edward's valiant defence throughout Committee impressed everyone. I was present throughout all of it, and my admiration for a true master of the House of Commons grew.

But, when all seemed set fair, along came Suez.

I had sensed that Edward did not see matters economic and social as completely with Rab's successor as Chancellor of the Exchequer, Harold Macmillan, as he had with Rab, but his resignation over Suez was a thunderbolt, of far greater significance than that of Anthony

Nutting, and a considerable shock to Eden. It so happened that I did not agree with him, and I was, as a Clerk, strictly neutral amidst the turmoil and bitterness that surged through the Palace of Westminster for those terrible days, but I admired his courage and integrity. Our first meeting was in the Members' Lobby, when he was standing very much alone. I spoke to him. I got the impression that he was very glad to speak to anyone, surrounded as he was by Conservatives who were cutting him dead. And that was the beginning of a very precious friendship, only ended by his death.

Of course, he was restored to office by Macmillan and rose to the Cabinet. He was, as Minister of Education, the pioneer of 'voluntary' comprehensives. But I felt that the gulf that had been opened between himself and certain bigotries in the then Conservative Party was incapable of being bridged. The Immigration Bill of 1968 was the final blow to a relationship that had gone sadly, and badly, sour. His decision to leave politics was of inestimable gain to Leeds University and higher education, but a disaster for the Conservative Party and the kind of decent, intelligent and sensitive liberal Toryism for which he stood.

In 1967, when a Fellow of All Souls, I organised a series of political seminars at the College, and among my guest speakers was Edward. My timing had been disastrous, as Schools were going on, when undergraduates' interest in politics is nil. But such was Edward's position that the room was packed, the students having come directly from the Examination Schools in their subfusc to hear him. He was, characteristically, acutely nervous, but he was brilliant. He described Hubert Henderson as 'the wisest of all economists' and explained why. His range of reading awed the undergraduates – and many of the dons. They loved him, and it was a triumph.

After the 1970 General Election, Robert Carr, for whom I had canvassed, now no longer on the sidelines, invited my wife and me to Glyndebourne for a memorable evening, and we met Edward there. Shortly afterwards he invited us. We began at his curious family mansion and then drove down with the Rees-Moggs. Edward loved games, and conceived one of a list of the 12 most odious British politicians of this century. We had to write them down separately on paper, and then compare them. The results were startlingly similar.

From 1972 until 1976 I was serving at the United Nations, and lost touch with Edward, as with so many other friends, and by the time I was an MP at the end of 1976 and later renewed my contact with him it was very clear that he was unwell. Only gradually did I realise how desperately ill he was, and on his visits to London to what he lightheartedly called 'my hotel' I used to have tea with him in the Lords, each time unhappily noting the inexorable physical decline, although mercifully the active brain was as sharp as ever.

One evening, when he was very frail, I virtually drove him into the Smoking Room of the House of Commons, plumped him down in a deep armchair and ordered him a huge whisky. There were many young Members around, of all parties, who literally did not recognise him. I told them quietly who he was, and very quickly he was in the midst of a group to whom he was only a name, but a deeply honoured one. He was in sparkling form, and I am sure enjoyed himself; his audience certainly did.

Only a few weeks later he was dead, his long battle over. Only a few months ago someone who was present came up to me in the Lobby of the Commons and said how grateful he was to me to have given him the opportunity of meeting Edward Boyle. I could only reply that it was Conservatives and public servants like Edward Boyle and Iain Macleod who had brought me into politics, and that it was a privilege for me, also, to have known him.

9

At the Education Ministry: An Official's View

Maurice Kogan

Our thinking about Edward Boyle's contribution to society, the width of his sympathies and interests, his unobtrusive command over so many complex and important aspects of national life, is still clouded by the early loss of a personality so compelling and magnanimous. The charm, generosity and capacity for friendship that so many experienced were in fact an integral part of Boyle's capacity to affect the wider scene. His influence was moral and charismatic as much as specific and direct.

Boyle came first to the Ministry of Education as Parliamentary Secretary when Harold Macmillan decided to bring him back into government after his principled stand over the policies that led to the Suez crisis. He had entered Parliament at the age of 27 in 1950 and very soon became a junior Minister at the Ministry of Supply in 1954. By the time he came to education at the beginning of 1957 he was 33 but had already put in just under two years in the prestigious post of Economic Secretary to the Treasury. The appointment had come over the tapes on a release from Number 10. He had left his post in government when on the way up, because, as he wrote to Anthony Eden in November 1956, 'I do not honestly feel that I can defend, as a Minister, the recent policy of the government.' The news of his appointment was greeted with delight in the Ministry of Education, a department not used to the cream of the political appointments system. He was a bachelor baronet, and an Etonian, with a reputation of high ability and moral courage.

I was his first private secretary at the Ministry of Education. Previous private secretaries in other departments had told us what to expect, that he was a delight to work with and his only fault a certain detachment from the ordinary routines that overtake starred ministers and ordinary folk alike: the need to get a haircut, to visit the dentist, or to deal with mail efficiently. He was very ably served at this time by his House of Commons Secretary, Shelagh Brown, and she kept him in order. But this did not prevent him from leaving quite large cheques uncashed in his back pocket. Nor did it stop him from leaving a ministerial red box in a taxi where it was found by some zealous army officer who promptly insisted on delivering it to the Secretary of State for War. None of this was in any sense an aristocratic disdain for the need to do what he promised. He always did that.

He was a marvellous teacher. He bought a vast number of books and read them quickly and then passed them on to me to read on train journeys. He wore a lot of learning lightly and assumed similar knowledge without condescension in others. He was entirely unstuffy.

In his relationships with civil servants he was fortunate in taking office when the Ministry of Education was led by an unusually gifted group including Toby Weaver, Antony Part, David Nenk, Derek Morrell and Ralph Fletcher, the last three of whom were to die while still under-secretaries. He admired their ability and offered the opinion that under-secretaries (three ranks down) at the Ministry of Education were of roughly the same quality as third secretaries (two levels down) at the Treasury, which he had just left.

In *The Politics of Education* he was clear that Ministers must lead: 'Ministers . . . belong to a party as well as a government and they are appointed with the responsibility of making clear what their value judgements are.' He dissented, however, from the lessons drawn from Hugh Dalton's account of Arthur Henderson's entry to the Foreign Office in 1929 that 'the first forty-eight hours decide whether a Minister is going to run his office, or whether his office is going to run him' and Dalton's own statement that a Minister should show his officials at the start that he has a mind of his own. Boyle never put up with overblown accounts of political verities and his retort was that 'I think that's one of those remarks, like Burke's letter to the electors of Bristol, which may get over-quoted in books on politics. . . . I would have thought it was more important in the early days for the civil servants to be clear whether they can have confidence in their Minister or not . . . civil servants want to know whether their Minister is going to be one of those that tends to get his way when there is collective discussion. Is he going to be one who knows clearly what he wants, what he is going after, and one whose reactions they can, in most cases, correctly anticipate? . . . But the idea that there is a sort of tussle for power on the first afternoon and that it's vital for the Minister to win, is an oversimplification.'

He defined the difference between the role of civil servants and ministers thus: 'The Minister has the absolute responsibility for showing what he is going for, to make clear what he is going for, how he wants to play the hand, and what are to him the most important objectives. The officials have got the equally important job of helping him by identifying the issues correctly. The idea that there is a sort of jujitsu going on on arrival, and that it is absolutely essential for a Minister to win the very first day, is taking one's eye off things that are more important. . . . '

He was also well aware – and both he and his interviewer (the present author) had the egregious Geoffrey Lloyd in mind – that 'departments make up or compensate for the deficiencies of their ministers remarkably well but, oh dear, some ministers can really lower morale quite quickly and easily.'

He thought the notion that 'there are predetermined and static suppositions within bureaucracy' was 'absolute and dangerous nonsense if only because new officials are coming to positions of authority and their value judgements are . . . a factor in the situation as well.'

It was on this fantasy-free and commonsensical approach to the respective roles of politicians and officials that he was able to build such good personal relationships. Civil servants enjoyed working with him and meeting him.

Boyle's underlying toughness was not perhaps greatly tested at the Ministry of Education because he shared the then overwhelming consensus on matters of policy. By 1962 hardly anybody was speaking out against expansion. The Robbins Report, published in 1963, was approved immediately by Sir Alec Douglas-Home's government; this legitimised the quadrupling of the proportion of the population entering higher education which was already well under way. The Conservatives at this time were still prepared to allow a gradual move towards comprehensive education. Indeed, Hugo Young (1989) has noted that Margaret Thatcher ten years later was still approving the establishment of comprehensive schools. When he first came to the Ministry and on his subsequent return there as Minister it can hardly be said that the Labour opposition had got its act together well enough to break the consensus. That came later, first in 1966, but even then the Secretary of State, Anthony Crosland, decided not to 'require' but only to 'request' local education authorities to move more wholeheartedly towards comprehensive education.

Had Boyle arrived in the 1980s it would have been entirely different. In this decade Ministers of Education have promoted policies which run against deeply continuous consensuses of the education world. As it was, almost everybody with whom Boyle was in contact – the senior administrators, HMIs, directors of education and most chairmen of education committees – were only concerned that the Ministry, or the DES as it became in 1964, should provide more of the same and faster. There was no educational equivalent of Suez.

What, then, were Edward Boyle's distinctive contributions to education? First, there were the policies for which he was responsible as Minister between 1962 and 1964. At that time he was responsible for accepting or approving or promoting policies which seemed both momentous and endurable. Many of them have been displaced by the radical conservative revolution of the 1980s. Thus he established the Ministry of Education's Curriculum Study Group and later sanctioned the creation of the Schools Council for the Curriculum and Examinations, in the hope that the Ministry of Education would become the centre of development shared with local education authorities and schools. Curriculum was a matter dear to his heart but he believed that it was best created by those who knew and worked with children and understood their educational needs rather than laid down from the centre.

The consensual mode implied in these developments are now all washed away. In his time the Anderson Committee reported on awards to students and it was on the basis of this that all local education authorities adopted national scales. But now the notion of full grants is to give way to part loans and the whole basis for funding higher education places to be radically altered. In his intervention in disputes between employers and teachers on salaries in 1963 he was, perhaps, nearer an anticipation of current styles. He approved a salary increase but did so by obtaining from Parliament a 'temporary power to settle salaries'. That power now seems embedded in rock. He started the Plowden and Gittins Committees on primary education and thus helped endorse the open and liberal modes of schooling and of curriculum development which are now seriously at a discount. He encouraged experiments in the organisation of secondary education and told the Association of Education Committees: 'We do no longer regard any pattern of organisation as the "norm" compared with which all others must be stigmatised.' This is, indeed, still a canon of Conservative policy, except that central preferences are more strongly asserted now. He announced the raising of the school leaving age to 16, to take place in 1970-1971.

It must have given him particular joy to welcome the recommendations of the Robbins Report which said that 'courses of higher education should be available for all of those who are qualified by ability and attainment to pursue them.' But in the 1980s the relatively qualified access of Robbins is likely to be abandoned in favour of wider access whilst, at the same time, higher education is placed under far more detailed control in deference to objectives set by government rather than by the academics themselves.

Edward Boyle did not originate many of these policies. Most had long been nourished in the womb of the Ministry of Education, the inspectorate and the policy community of local authorities and the other major interests with which the Ministry worked. His contribution was not so systematic and determined as that of Anthony Crosland, who had published his views on many educational issues before reaching office and who had a clear belief in strengthening the planning system within the DES.

His role was charismatic and moral rather than that of an outstanding policy innovator. But if Edward Boyle was somewhat less of an originator than either Eccles or Crosland, he changed the ethos, level and style of discourse within which policies were made. He put his enormous authority behind such themes as the widening of opportunity in society and increasing the level of civilisation for all citizens. He staunchly supported policies, even if he did not invent them, which would compensate for the inequality of home environment of children over the country; and in his Foreword to the Newsom Report in 1963 he said that 'the essential point is that all children should have an equal opportunity of acquiring intelligence, and developing their talents to the full.' He sponsored 'positive discrimination' in education which was promoted in the Plowden Report (1967). In this he was moving to the edge of Conservative policy in a way that then seemed possible within the party.

Boyle, therefore legitimised the expansion of education and other social services, even if these policies were in a sense ready made for him when he came to the Ministry. He knew what his objectives were and was concerned that the opportunity state should become real and that education should improve freedom of choice as well as wealth. In this the centre would establish major policies which would rest on the values established by Ministers. But control of the schools should rest with local education authorities and the institutions themselves.

Edward Boyle thought that policies in education were different from some other subjects in that they originated overwhelmingly from the education world, from 'the logic of the education service as it was developing'.

He exemplified ways in which a Minister could be undogmatic and free of rigid moralistic commitments to Conservative or any other ideology and back the best policy on their arguments and merits. He told the Party Conference in 1968: 'I will join with you in the fight against socialist dogmatism wherever it rears its head. But do not ask me to oppose it with an equal or opposite Conservative dogma, because in education it is the dogmatism itself which is wrong.'

On some issues he took a firm line and made a strong contribution. Teacher supply problems never seemed to go away; he described them as being based on 'the economics of Passchendaele', because one was forever creating teacher training places for young women who then left to have their families. He insisted on maintaining the timing for raising the school-leaving age and, as we have observed, he shared officials' impatience with the fan dance that constituted salary negotiations between the local authority and teacher associations. He was not prepared to accept Conservative dogma on comprehensive and non-streamed schools. He believed in curriculum development and in eradicating the baleful effect of external examinations, now to be restored with bells on them, on the curriculum. He used his position from within the party to advance the claims of an expanding maintained system to the middle class voter and to his own party.

In his own words: 'the norm of opinion by 1965 was clearly on Robbins' side [that is, on the side of expansion] and not on Bantock's [that is, the view that "anybody of real ability can now make the grade"].' He claimed that he 'did something to bring "middle opinion" over to this side, to make it plain that the norm of opinion had shifted.'

A minister concerned to express wholesome values and to encourage others can only do this through the patient application of persuasive skills. When he first came to the Ministry as a junior minister he had too little to do, even though he took all of the House of Commons business because the Minister, Lord Hailsham, was in the House of Lords.

He had to resolve opposed compulsory purchase orders, the closure of village schools and – a task which he undertook with care, decency and interest – the cases of teachers reported for unprofessional behaviour which might lead to their disqualification.

Other issues before him as Parliamentary Secretary were relatively secondary, although he dealt with a stream of parliamentary questions, adjournment debates and the committee stage defence of the 1958 Local Government Bill. This led him to consider, in discussions which we had many times together, what his role might be. The clue came characteristically from a review written by a friend of his, Michael Howard, of Lord Templewood's *Empire of the Air* (1957). Howard perceptively noted how Templewood (then Samuel Hoare) when Secretary of State for Air had 'set out to make the Air Force smart'. Howard wrote 'the basic reason why our state educational system, on paper one of the finest in the world, has failed to create equality of opportunity is that no Minister of Education has ever really attempted to win for it, in realistic social terms, parity of esteem. It was not enough, in this absurd country, to make state schools efficient; they should have also been made smart. . . . ' Boyle therefore made an enormous programme of visits to schools, local authorities and other educational establishments and responded unstintingly to requests for speeches out of London. In these he set out to encourage teachers and parents to believe in the benign influence and efficacy of the maintained school system. He influenced people not only through speeches but also through more informal discourse; not all of those who were delighted to meet him over dinner were prepared for some of his defence of liberal principles as they entertained him with what they thought would be posh chatter.

How does his substantive contribution, and contribution to the style of government, compare with that of present ministers? Boyle was not representative of ministers of his time; they included their share of opportunists, authoritarians, the industrious and the idle. But his style would have differed strongly from that of even the ablest ministers of our time. He believed that the Ministry of Education should lead the educational system, but he also believed profoundly in the merits of discussion, discourse and, where possible, consensus. The difference between Boyle and current Conservative education ministers is that he was consensual and charismatic whereas they are heroic in their assumptions about the power they should wield and the way that they should wield it.

Secondly, he viewed the operation of the free market, particularly in social welfare, with distinctly modified rapture. He was wholeheartedly behind the expansion of the consumer society and, indeed, regarded education as part of it. He was all for freedom of choice, and for the expansion of choice.

His behaviour as Minister is well explained by an essay published well after he left office (Schilpp, 1974). The essay is charmingly written and displays an acuity and, in places, adversarial toughness that disposes of any notion that Boyle was 'soft' either intellectually or emotionally. He applauded Popper's *Open Society* because when he first read it as an undergraduate he discovered a book dedicated to the values of 'humaneness' and 'reasonableness'. 'These are the values which, above all others, seem to me at the heart of what we mean when we speak of "a civilised society".' He admired Popper because he would not allow either power or 'the admiration of brilliance' or 'the greatness and uniqueness of medieval craftsmanship' to rank higher than humanitarianism. He quoted with approval John Stuart Mill that 'a man for whom awe automatically excites admiration may be aesthetically developed, but he is morally uncultivated.'

In discussing Popper and his emphasis on piecemeal social engineering, in opposition to utopian planning, he showed disdain for those who believe that the economy could be run as in wartime and who had a deterministic belief in 'the onward march of socialism'. At the same time, he found himself equally divided from those who advocated a more authoritarian approach to questions of individual and social morality and 'who failed to realise the implications of the great change that had come over our society, once for all, during the Second World War when public policy had come to accept a far "stronger" definition of the good of all.' And so he welcomed Popper's anti-authoritarianism and his acceptance of the necessity for institutions, coupled with his rejection of unthinking deference towards them. He saw in Popper's emphasis on 'reputability' the crucial importance of learning from our own mistakes, and the realisation that 'truth, so far from being manifest, is hard to come by'. Such a creed leaves little room for conviction politics.

In this essay, many things that Edward Boyle had said to me in the course of fragmentary conversations came together. In the terms expressed there, one could begin to understand why, although a Conservative and an anti-Socialist, he had no difficulty in advancing the cause of social welfare through publicly maintained institutions as well as through the expansion of consumer choice in the free market. It gives the clue to his attitude towards public authorities which some might consider subordinate to central government and to the hundreds of thousands of teachers working, for not much pay, in tens of thousands of schools. The lack of condescension and the belief in others' power to do good were part of the 'humaneness' and 'reasonableness' that he so admired in Popper.

References

Edward Boyle, 'Karl Popper's *Open Society*: A Personal Appreciation', in Paul A. Schilpp (ed.), *The Philosophy of Karl Popper*, Book 2, La Salle, Illinois, 1974.

Maurice Kogan, Edward Boyle and Anthony Crosland, *The Politics of Education*, Penguin Education, 1971.

10

At the Education Ministry: His Junior Minister's View

Christopher Chataway

In the summer of 1962 I was summoned by the Prime Minister and invited to become Parliamentary Secretary at the Ministry of Education. In keeping with the courteous old world style he cultivated, Harold Macmillan spent a full twenty minutes on the interview with a prospective junior minister of no importance, despite the fact that this was the 'night of the long knives' in which he was making wholesale changes at every level of his administration. He explained to me some of the reasons why he was getting rid of so many of his senior colleagues. Elaborating upon his points of difference with Selwyn Lloyd, until then the Chancellor of the Exchequer, he would pause every so often – much to my alarm – to enquire about my views. I was 31, had been an MP for just over two years and was surprised to find myself elevated to such giddy heights. Towards the end of the discussion he told me that I should be working for Sir Edward Boyle who was to replace Lord Eccles as Minister for Education.

Edward had written me a kind note of congratulation on my maiden speech, in which I had tried to deploy some progressive ideas about race relations, but I had spoken with him only a few times. I admired most of his liberal views. He seemed, however, to be rather a peculiar sort of individual and I heard the news that he was to be my boss with no particular feelings one way or the other.

When asked to contribute to this book more than a quarter of a century later, I realised with some surprise that even now hardly a week goes by without my recalling something or other that he said during the two years that I spent with him in Education. His influence upon me was profound, as I suspect it was upon most of those with whom he worked closely.

In 1962 the Ministry of Education, which was without the responsibility subsequently assumed by the Department of Education and

Science for universities and for science, had just two ministers. We must have seemed a strangely ill-assorted couple. I had been an Olympic runner only five or six years before and I must still have looked and moved like an athlete. Edward was very fat and obviously ill co-ordinated. Although only 38 he had many of the attributes of an elderly professor, and even when hurrying he bustled along without a trace of youth left in his stride.

He could in the right environment be marvellously articulate. He could also be gauche and ill at ease. Despite his baronetcy and his Eton education, he was painfully lacking in some of the social graces. He could flush with embarrassment and his bitten finger-nails bore witness to some internal tensions.

A few years later, just as most of his contemporaries were trying to give up, he tried to start smoking as a sort of nail-protecting diversionary tactic. Although already an obviously confirmed bachelor, he once made clear to me that his inclinations were heterosexual and with attractive women he often seemed to be particularly ill at ease.

Edward's style of conversation was unique and could be disconcerting. Rather than embarking as most people do upon some exploratory chatter with a view to finding a topic of mutual interest, Edward would plunge straight into a chosen subject. Whether it was music or history or literature, he would within a minute or two be deep into some abstruse debate, apparently oblivious of the fact that those with whom he was ostensibly in conversation were often quite unable to contribute.

Had one noticed in the most recent edition of *Encounter* that so and so had produced this new theory about the role of Ophelia, but surely it hardly dealt with the very powerful argument deployed so many years ago by such and such a critic which Edward felt – didn't you? – was still, despite its occasionally strident assertiveness, the best analysis of *Hamlet*?

A casual reference to Drake or the Armada could produce from Edward a rapid review of all the rival theories about the battle apparently proceeding upon the assumption that you were as familiar with the various historians as he was.

Was this showing off or one-upmanship? Was it evidence of insensitivity? Did he genuinely not notice that most people he met knew so much less than he did about most things? I rapidly came to the conclusion that it was none of this. It was more a bubbling over of intellectual excitement. He just felt that it was much more interesting to be surveying the frontiers of knowledge than paddling about in some lazy backwater.

He was never contemptuous or dismissive of others. There was no condescension about him. He seemed to start from the assumption that other human beings were just as capable as he of being interested in the things he found fascinating, just as capable of enjoying what gave him pleasure. He also had a well justified confidence in his own ability to communicate to others his interests and enthusiasms.

He would arrive at the office about 10 a.m. In an interview several years later, when Vice-Chancellor of Leeds, he said he wished that it had been earlier. It was only a few years before, however, that Geoffrey Lloyd, reared in more leisurely pre-war days, rarely appeared in the Ministry before lunch. The early morning gatherings of Ministers initiated by Peter Walker as the first Secretary of State for the giant Department of the Environment for 'verbal calisthenics', in the sardonic phrase of one permanent secretary, were all in the future.

It is difficult to imagine that Edward's grasp of the job could have been further improved by any earlier start. Very little in the Ministry or in the education world outside escaped his scrutiny. He read voraciously and fast. He could absorb information from discussion just as surely and speedily. The depths of his knowledge about any subject which interested him and for which he had responsibility were formidable.

I always looked forward to departmental meetings chaired by Edward and particularly to the internal meetings. A large part of a minister's life is taken up by deputations which have come to complain or make representations about this or that. It is mostly ritual since both sides know very well what the other is going to say.

Edward would carry off these sort of meetings with style, reacting with asperity if the complainants were offensive,but generally sending a deputation away reluctantly captivated by his sincerity, his encyclopaedic knowledge and his wit, even where the answer had been a predictably firm no.

Much more entertaining, though, were the meetings within the Department called to discuss specific problems or issues. Edward would often invite quite junior officials to such gatherings. From his previous experience as Parliamentary Secretary in the Ministry, he knew many of the principals and assistant secretaries. Not only did he know their names and faces, but he knew also a great deal about their views and abilities.

It was a pool of knowledge to which he was always adding and once he had extracted information about an individual's opinions, or experience or background, it was filed away and his mind's retrieval systems never seemed to fail to locate such facts when required. When discussing some policy issue with him, a building proposal maybe in the North-West, he would ask whether I was aware that young so-and-so, a civil servant in his late twenties perhaps, had strong views on the matter. 'He is a socialist of course, but was brought up on Merseyside and he has a good analytical mind.'

At the meetings Edward would always try and usually succeed in getting all the participants to give their own individual views without equivocation, and irrespective either of what their superior's position might be or of what they might expect the Minister wanted to hear.

The preparatory meetings before Question Time or before a debate always demonstrated the care and attention he gave to the House. He would try out answers or lines of argument, rolling phrases around for inspection and joining in the laughter if anyone effectively punctured one of his trial balloons.

'I am not a punishing debater,' he once said to me in the course of assessing his strengths and weaknesses as a Commons performer. It was an understatement. Although his defences were hard to penetrate, he never seemed even to try to land political punches. It was not that he disapproved of aggressive political oratory. He admired it in others, but it was not his style.

I never remember him, therefore, scoring a political triumph in the House. But he was almost invariably a good performer. He could hold the attention of the House by the quality of his exposition and above all by his honesty. People would listen to him because they knew that his words were always his own, would indicate clearly what he really thought and were invariably the product of considerable preparation.

One of Edward's most important political hallmarks was the care with which he would assemble the arguments on either side of an important issue. He would attempt to defer judgement until he had gathered in the views from high and low within government and outside.

He did not want just to be able to list in his mind the arguments for and against. He wanted to get inside them, to understand their strengths and the feelings that surrounded them. He wanted really to comprehend the emotions generated by an issue in the breasts of supporters and opponents alike. It was a process that could sometimes lead the observer to believe that Edward was indecisive.

One example of an issue on which he encouraged debate, but refused to come to any very definite conclusion, was secondary reorganisation. Soon after my arrival at the Ministry, I remember seeing a minute in which he described his attitude to the matter as eclectic.

As it happened I was none too sure at the time what the word meant. When I got to a dictionary and discovered that it must in the context mean choosing the best from both the comprehensive and the grammar/secondary modern systems, I was not much the wiser. Were we in favour of the 11-plus or against it?

It turned out to be all a little more complicated than that. Edward's thinking developed cautiously. If he had been bent upon political advancement there is no question as to which side he should have thrown his weight. The grammar schools were very popular in the Conservative Party.

Relatively few Conservative MPs then took much interest in education and, since nearly all had been to private schools themselves, most knew very little about the maintained system. One remarkable example of this detachment from our preoccupations in the Ministry of Education occurred in relation to the timing of examinations. Some powerful arguments, which I cannot now recall, had been marshalled in favour of holding examinations early in the year which might result in the summer school holidays starting in June and ending in August.

Edward was summoned by the Chairman of the 1922 Committee, a very important person in whom still waters were believed to run extremely deep, principally because he hardly ever said anything. The whole idea, he told Edward with a quite surprising passion, was out of the question. If the State Schools changed the date of their term times, Eton might have to do the same and then young men would find themselves at school during the grouse shooting.

Having no intention of altering the school dates anyway, Edward was able to give the strongest assurances, while struggling hard to keep a straight face, that in settling this important educational issue, he would never forget the Glorious Twelfth.

On the subject of grammar schools, though, he resolutely refused to say what most active Conservatives wanted to hear. It was a stand which cost him much support in the party both during the Macmillan government and to an even greater extent later in the 1960s, when he refused in opposition to launch an assault on Anthony Crosland's famous circular 10/65 which accelerated the move away from the 11-Plus.

Edward could feel and sympathise with the emotions aroused on both sides of the argument. I can remember him coming back from a visit to some boys' grammar school deeply impressed by the ethos, the discipline and the evident commitment to excellence.

It was obvious, as he described the eager faces, the uniforms and the conversations he had had with boys and staff, that he had no difficulty in understanding and indeed sharing the profound attachment of so many to the traditional British grammar school. And yet he could see too the injustice and the waste caused by a system which tried to divide children at the age ten (because the 11-plus exam was taken at the age of ten) into two types, which for all the tactful circumlocution might just as well be called the clever and the stupid.

Edward realised that the 11-plus system was the egalitarianism of the 1920s and the 1930s – a way of selecting the 'able poor'. The research evidence from a number of countries was accumulating to show that it was a very uncertain method of allocating benefits. Intelligence was a much more complicated commodity than people had once thought. Far too many children were being allowed to write themselves off below their true level of ability.

In his introduction to the report of the Newsom Committee on secondary education, Edward wrote: 'the essential point is that all children should have an equal opportunity of acquiring intelligence and developing their talents and abilities to the full.' At one of the leading education conferences in 1963, Edward said that separate schools at 11 should no longer be regarded as the norm with everything else looked upon as experimental.

All this was hardly a clarion call to anything, but it represented a significant change of policy for the Conservative Party. It was always a posture from which it would be difficult to score many political runs – either for the party or for Edward. His cautious and apparently agnostic position did not win him many plaudits. The supporters of reorganisation were unimpressed by his hesitancy, while the defenders of the grammar school had the distinct impression that a pass was about to be sold. Edward spent much time and effort in explaining his position within the party and in attempting to neutralise opposition.

It would have been easy for a less thoughtful or a less honest Minister to have led the party into outright opposition against reorganisation, which could have entrenched the rigidities of the 11-plus in many areas and produced in many others the chaos of schools being merged and demerged as local educational authorities changed back and forth between Labour and Conservative.

If Edward had continued to have responsibility for education, he would almost certainly have discouraged the makeshift schemes which gave so little chance of success to many comprehensives. He would surely not have pushed all the direct grant grammar schools into the independent sector.

He was strongly supporting experiments with middle schools, and it may be that this is the direction in which his policy would have evolved. Such schools could have provided the opportunity to delay selection until 13 or 14. The best of the grammar schools could have found a place as academic senior high schools or sixth form colleges. The country would certainly have benefited from a more evolutionary approach.

Edward's interest extended to every part of the Ministry. Although he delegated to me responsibility for many of the time-consuming appeals procedures relating to school closures, compulsory purchase orders, morally unsatisfactory teachers and appeals from parents against a variety of local education authority decisions, he was always willing to involve himself as deeply as required in any particularly difficult or important case.

It was always a pleasure to me when he would drop into my office, lower himself into a chair, tell me what had gone on in Cabinet, bring me up to date on gossip in the higher echelons of government, and give his advice on any thorny problems that I might raise with him. He spent a lot of time visiting schools and colleges and much of his astonishingly wide knowledge of every aspect of the education service was derived from outside the Ministry. His visits were not confined to the locations in which he would most obviously shine. Although most people would have perceived the Senior Common Room as Edward's natural milieu, he would go to talk to youth clubs in tough city neighbourhoods – and succeed in getting a good hearing.

In the two years from 1962 to 1964 important advances were made in curriculum development, teacher supply, the modernisation of old schools and the development of further education. This is not the place, nor am I the right person, to attempt a comprehensive assessment of his contribution as Minister of Education and then Minister of State in the newly formed Department of Education and

Science. This voluntary demotion marked, however, one of his most important legacies to the education service. It arose from the report of the Robbins Committee in October 1963.

The fact that the government announced its acceptance of the main Robbins proposals within 24 hours of the report's publication owed much to Edward. Responsibility for the universities had just been passed from the Treasury to Quintin Hogg as Lord President, but it was probably Edward who argued most strongly for university expansion. He realised that rising standards in the schools were making it progressively harder to gain entry to universities.

So many years later when we still have a smaller proportion of young people in higher education than most other developed countries, it is hard to remember how fiercely the expansion of the universities was resisted. 'More means worse' was the slogan on which *The Times* campaigned and was widely supported. The Macmillan government, when Selwyn Lloyd was still at the Treasury, had had a public confrontation with the University Grants Committee two years earlier over money and numbers. So it was certainly no mean achievement to secure from the government so quick and unqualified a commitment to the Robbins principle that 'courses of higher education should be available for all those who are qualified by ability and attainment to pursue them and who wish to do so.' It meant almost a doubling of students within ten years.

The second achievement – and it was one in which Edward played an even larger part – was to overcome the Robbins recommendation that responsibility in government for higher education should remain separate from the schools. With the support of an important minority of Vice-Chancellors, Edward successfully argued for the creation of the Department of Education and Science, urging upon Sir Alec Home as Prime Minister that Quintin Hogg should be the Secretary of State and that he should continue to have responsibility for schools within the Department as Minister of State. It was unquestionably the right decision, but I have little doubt that if Edward had argued for his own political advantage it would not have been taken.

The government's days were now numbered. In advance of the 1964 election, which Harold Wilson was narrowly to win, it was arranged that some ten Cabinet ministers would make speeches on the same day in different parts of the country on the theme of the nuclear deterrent. Labour's two greatest weaknesses were regarded as nationalisation and unilateralism and this particular exercise was designed to highlight the defence issue.

Edward's preparations for the speech were remarkable. He consulted defence experts inside and outside Whitehall. He virtually constructed his own private defence policy from scratch and tailored his remarks accordingly. As he continued to work on the subject over the preceding weeks, I argued in vain that the speech was hardly worth the trouble since with ten Ministers speaking on the same subject on the same day, it was extremely unlikely that Edward would even get reported except in a few local papers. Why not do, as everyone else does, and on subjects that are not one's own, take the party line and use the material from Central Office? It would all be good stuff for a rousing political speech, which was what was required. I was right that not a word about Edward's speech appeared in any national newspaper. I really knew him well enough by then, however, to know that my advice was certain to go unheeded. The level at which he always attempted to conduct political argument did not allow a distinction between occasions or subjects where one expected to be judged on every word, and others where one simply performed as a party politician.

In his long interview with Maurice Kogan published in 1971 (*The Politics of Education*), Edward made it clear that he left the House of Commons in part because he realised that he was unlikely to secure any of the top three or four jobs. That was almost certainly a correct assessment. Considerations of political advantage, whether personal or party, just did not rate highly enough with Edward to give him much of a chance of getting to the very top.

Had he stayed in politics – or as a peer returned to politics – he would not have been Prime Minister or Chancellor of the Exchequer. He probably would not have been Foreign Secretary or Home Secretary. He could have been a brilliant Leader of the Commons. In whatever capacity he served he would have continued by his example to make all those around him think more deeply and more dispassionately about issues. As it was, his contribution to public life, though sadly abbreviated, was unique.

11

A Cabinet Colleague
John Boyd-Carpenter

One could not meet Edward Boyle without at once realising that one was in the presence of a good man. It was impossible to imagine him doing anything which he knew was wrong, or even dubious. This is the stiffest criterion of character. But manifestly what was wrong, and what was shabby, in conduct repelled him. He disliked it in others; he would not tolerate it in himself.

Not that he was either censorious or a prig. But this sensitivity to even the hint of wrongdoing showed itself with brutal clarity at the time of the Suez crisis. As Economic Secretary to the Treasury he was not at all involved in the business; in fact knowledge of what was going on was confined to the little group of collaborators whom Sir Anthony Eden had gathered round him. But from what he knew he could see that wrong was being done, and regardless of the effect on his political career he resigned because he refused to remain a member of a government which was so conducting itself. Others of us at the time took a less high-principled line, and a less dramatic view of what Sir Anthony Eden was doing. We were pretty sure he was being silly – particularly in the way he was treating President Eisenhower and the United States – but also knew that because of the way in which he was handling it we did not know the full story. I remember discussing the question of resignation with Walter Monckton, until recently Minister of Defence and still a member of the Cabinet. He said he had no idea of what was going on, but had no intention of resigning. He pointed out to me that those of us who were not at that time Cabinet members had even less reason so to do.

This episode is worth recalling for the vivid light it throws on Edward's character. He would not remain in any capacity in a government which he thought was doing wrong although in circumstances and in a way for which he had no responsibility, and in a context of which he knew little. It is to Edward's credit, and to that of Eden's successor, Harold Macmillan, that it did not do serious damage to his political career.

But there were many other sides to Edward. He was an intellectual in the strictest construction of the word. His intellect was powerful and it was backed by an astonishing memory, and he was extremely well read.

A major influence in his life was his mother Beatrice. She was a woman of strong character whom an early widowhood had caused to develop considerable powers of independent management. She had a proper admiration for her son's abilities. But she also maintained firm control over his domestic life. She managed their home in Sussex firmly and efficiently. Meals and domestic staff were well organised; she took full charge of his domestic needs and gave him orderly domestic comfort. But it is often the case that men with mothers who look after their needs so well do not marry. Their lives seem complete without it. So it was with Edward. Life was organised and directed with a standard of comfort far beyond the expectations of any bachelor.

He was certainly not an ascetic. He enjoyed good and lively company, particularly of clever people. And he greatly enjoyed good food and wine. I used to lunch with him from time to time at the Connaught Hotel. This was one of the best restaurants in London. We used to sit over a splendid and prolonged lunch, and put the world and our colleagues to rights. He was immensely good company, witty if tolerant, and these were occasions I greatly valued. But it must be admitted that my work on those afternoons was less dynamic than it should have been.

His way of life in the country was similar. My wife and I stayed one July weekend with Edward and his mother at their home in Sussex. The weather was perfect, the house had a tennis court, and the sea was not far off. These amenities attracted me with thought of outdoor activities appropriate to a summer weekend in the country. But Edward was not to be moved by hints. To direct suggestions he replied that the tennis court was not in very good order, and that it was not a very nice bit of beach. In the event, although we lunched and dined magnificently, and the conversation was stimulating, the nearest I got to open-air exercise was walking with Edward up and down the lawn in front of the house after lunch on Sunday, discussing the state of the nation and our colleagues.

His friendly and unpompous manner made him very popular in the House of Commons where he sat for twenty years as member for the Handsworth division of Birmingham. And his kindness and helpfulness to individuals made him very popular in the constituency.

He never snubbed people and his obviously genuine feeling for people in trouble was much appreciated.

He much enjoyed being Minister of Education. Education was a thing he really cared about. And while in this post he finally announced the long-delayed step of moving the school-leaving age from 15 to 16. This was a not uncontroversial decision. Some people questioned, and still question, the desirability or wisdom of keeping non-academic young people in conventional schools for another year at an age when they feel themselves to be grown-up. But Edward dismissed these doubters as old-fashioned reactionaries and felt strongly that the extra year at school would help to advance equality of opportunity among young people. This was a major decision about which he had neither doubts nor hesitations.

Edward took very seriously his duties as a member of the Cabinet in 1962–64. His interventions were quietly spoken, brief and to the point. He did *not* get into arguments with his colleagues unless compelled by circumstances, or by them, so to do. He was, however, involved in one incident through no choice of his own. As Chief Secretary to the Treasury, responsible for public expenditure, I had to discuss each of my colleagues' proposed annual Estimates for the forthcoming year. It was generally possible to settle differences of view, mainly as to the amount of public spending to be permitted, in discussions and by negotiation. If agreement was *not* reached the issues went to a Cabinet Committee, and if no agreement was reached there (which was very rare) the matter came back to Cabinet for discussion. On one occasion Quintin Hogg, who was Minister for Education and Science, refused to discuss his Estimates. He said: 'These are my Estimates. I decline to discuss them.' I had no option but to say that I was not prepared in these circumstances to agree them, and if Mr Hogg persisted in his refusal to follow the normal procedure, no Estimate for his department would be approved.

The matter then came to Cabinet. After some rather explosive discussion, the Prime Minister asked Edward Boyle to take over discussion on the Education Department's behalf. This he reluctantly agreed to do. Discussions then followed, first between officials of the two departments in the usual way, and then between Edward and me. After clear if firm discussions we arrived at a compromise. Thus Education Estimates were reduced without any harm being done to the Education service, but with some saving to public funds. We came to a clear agreement which we reported to Cabinet.

Edward was a good person with whom to negotiate: clear, polite, moderate, fair in essentials and with a readiness to compromise.

He was at all stages of his career highly and happily gregarious. He was a member of the Carlton Club, of the Athenaeum, of Pratts and of the Beefsteak. Each of these satisfied one side of his character. At that time all major Conservative figures and Cabinet members were members of the Carlton and most of them lunched there regularly at the parliamentary table. Harold Macmillan as Prime Minister lunched there two or three times a week during the parliamentary session. The Athenaeum, then as now, was the London club most used by senior academics and intellectuals, although it was not particularly lively and the fare tended towards austerity. Pratts, owned by the Duke of Devonshire, was a venue for late and cheerful evenings, and the Beefsteak was similar in a more old-fashioned and restrained way. Edward as a bachelor found that his clubs played a very important role in his life. And he was popular in all of them. After he moved to the Vice-Chancellor's residence at Leeds they became an even more important link for him with the London world which he continued to frequent and enjoy.

His cultural interests ranged widely. They were indicated by his trusteeship of the British Museum and his practical interest in many artistic efforts. And he retained till the end of his life his concern with the major issues of public affairs. He was not only a trustee of the Pilgrim Trust – which has done so much on the vital question of Anglo-American relations – but also of the Ditchley Foundation, where also much has been done to help and guide the same close relationship.

In these ways he ensured that his residence in the north did not cut him off from the major issues and major figures of public life. These interests he retained until his unhappily premature death. This was not only a great loss to his many friends, but also a very real one to the country and to public life.

> He nothing common did, or mean,
> Upon that memorable scene.

12

A Supporter of Friends and Causes

Edward Heath

Edward Boyle had a remarkable gift for friendship, particularly with the young. Extending beyond people it also embraced organisations and institutions as well as artistic activities of every kind.

Those who knew him best appreciated that his likes and dislikes were not based on background or class, nor on intellectual capacity or a particular skill, though he did at times find it difficult to tolerate what he would term crass stupidity. He rested his judgement on what he considered to be the genuine nature of the activities, the innate honesty of those concerned, to which and to whom he was extending his friendship.

This meant that his relationships were long and enduring. It explains why he is so widely missed. He had no difficulty in getting to terms with those who differed from him, so long as they were not seeking to destroy the very foundations of this faith, tolerance and respect for the views of others. Within these bounds his friends knew that they could always rely on his loyal support.

To the outside world his outstanding characteristic was undoubtedly his gentleness of approach, whether greeting strangers, speaking on a public platform, arguing his case from the despatch box in the House of Commons, handling a confrontational situation with students at his university or discussing a less than adequate performance in an interval at the Opera. But it would have been a gross misjudgement for anyone to deduce that his courtesy and understanding were a cover for weakness or vacillation. At every test he displayed frankness and integrity of a high order. His resignation from the government at the time of the Suez crisis demonstrated his quiet resolve.

His constituency was not an easy one to hold or to manage. Many of his voters disagreed with him on such basic questions as capital punishment and other ethical issues. But they supported him because of his obvious concern for their individual welfare and the life of their community. They respected him and responded to his friendliness.

Perhaps, as time passed, he found the House of Commons more and more difficult for his own nature to continue to assimilate. To begin with he enjoyed to the full the spirit of fraternity which pervades the exchanges in the corridors, the smoking room, the tea room and the library, so different from that which exists on the floor of the Chamber. But later, with front bench responsibility for controversial subjects, the often narrow-minded party approach on both sides dismayed him. Although he was always happy with his beloved educational matters he lost the desire to move higher up the hierarchy into less attractive fields, even though he realised it was necessary if he were to fulfil the promise seen in him many years earlier as 'a future Prime Minister'.

As colleagues in the Cabinet and the Shadow Cabinet we all admired his industry, his lucidity in exposition, his constructive approach and his manifold interests in life. The Conservative Party in the country was not so appreciative. The proceedings at the annual party conference were obviously distasteful to him and he rarely adjusted himself to them.

Thus, when opportunity offered, he left the mainstream of politics for the Vice-Chancellorship of Leeds University. He abandoned the central administration of education in favour of carrying out the practical task of influencing those engaged in it, both as teachers and as students. So successful was he in extending the hand of friendship to both that during some of the most difficult years in our universities since the end of the Second World War, the early 1970s, including the bitter controversy of the Vietnam War, he guided Leeds University quietly through those tumultuous times to a secure and rewarding peaceful existence. This established his influence over his fellow Vice-Chancellors and reinforced his authority over the political powers concerned with his other interests, such as the Vice-Chancellors' Committee and the Review Body on Top Salaries.

Nowhere was his gift of friendship more strongly shown than in his love of the arts, especially music, supported by a wide and detailed knowledge which almost entitled him to the description of musicologist. That his death prevented him from writing his book on Fauré, for which he had been collecting material for so long, is a lamentable loss to the musical world.

A Supporter of Friends and Causes

Dearest of all aspects of his friendship was Edward's concern for his friends. His attention to their interests was constant, his support for them personally was always unquestioned, his hospitality was most generous, at his small parties he was witty and stimulating: in brief he was a most civilised man.

13

The Move Away from Politics
William Rees-Mogg

The winter of 1946 was not as cold as the frozen winter of 1947, but it was cold enough. There was very little fuel, and we sat around in the Oxford Union in our overcoats, warming our hands at little paraffin heaters. The debates, however, were of remarkable quality for an undergraduate debating society at any time.

Of course, the undergraduates were a great deal more mature than undergraduates usually are. I had come up straight from school, but most of my Oxford contemporaries had come back from wartime experiences of one kind or another. The most distinguished Labour speakers in the Union were Tony Crosland and Tony Wedgwood Benn. The most distinguished Conservative speaker was Edward Boyle.

The impression Edward then left was one of an authority disproportionate to his years. We could never, even those of us who really were his contemporaries in age, fully regard him as a contemporary. He had an intellectual maturity we did not possess. He had read more widely, he had thought more deeply, he had considered issues at a level more profound than ours. There was then no suggestion that this thinking had brought him to the left of the Conservative Party.

The character he thus presented was more like that of the great Lord Salisbury, traditional in political issues but intellectual in approach to politics. Admittedly he was concerned to distinguish between those parts of the Conservative traditions which deserved to be preserved, and those parts which were better discarded, or were indefensible, but he was, as all Conservatives were, in reaction against the Labour victory of 1945, by no means a believer in the Fabian socialism of the Attlee government. Inside the Oxford Conservatives, who included Margaret Roberts, he was a central figure, certainly in no way left of centre.

It was his intellectual maturity which we followed. He seemed at that point to be the natural political leader of his generation. People spoke of him, without the reservations that were to come later, as a probable future Prime Minister and, if not that, as someone whose judgement was so sure that he was certain to be a dominant figure in Conservative politics in his lifetime. When he got his celebrated third we all blamed it, without hesitation, on the examiners, and I still have no doubt that we were right to do so. It is the examiners' job to discover who the best candidates are.

I think we would have noted that he was not the tidiest of administrators. What real intellectual is? But bodies seemed to thrive under his benign leadership, whether the Union or the Conservative Association.

What then went wrong with his political career? Or perhaps one should say, what went right? There is certainly the question of ambition. When he was an undergraduate, Edward Boyle shared the common view of his potential future. He hoped, and probably expected, to hold high office in the Conservative Party, higher office than he ever held in fact. He knew that he had a particular authority with his contemporaries, that they saw him not just as an able man, as one might have seen Iain Macleod or Reginald Maudling, but as a wise man, which is a different and more important thing. At that stage he wanted to get into Parliament, he wanted to reach junior office, he wanted to reach senior office. I do not know that he aimed to be Prime Minister – he would have thought it silly to fantasise about so remote a possibility – but he must have known that no-one would be surprised if even that was to come his way.

The early stages of his career put him ahead of his contemporaries. An election fight in Perry Barr, a safe Labour seat; adoption for Handsworth, then a safe Conservative seat; membership of the Birmingham caucus which Geoffrey Lloyd had taken over from Neville Chamberlain; early promotion to Economic Secretary to the Treasury, in succession to Reginald Maudling, under the friendly and admiring patronage of Rab Butler – these in the early and mid-1950s were the natural first steps of a distinguished political career. Edward loved the Treasury. He became closely intellectually involved in the problems of post-war economic recovery, and in the Treasury's efforts to develop economic policies which would expand and strengthen the British economy. He believed, or came to believe, in a neo-Keynesian view of these problems, but he was not a mere disciple of any school.

Already in the mid-1950s some of the characteristics of Britain's post-war economic difficulties had become apparent: stop-go economics, a certain tendency to inflation, a relatively disappointing performance by international standards. In retrospect one could say that Edward's economic views were too much influenced by the academic economists and senior Treasury civil servants whom he most respected. His experience of a Birmingham constituency had not at all converted him to a businessman's view of economic theory. Yet perhaps it was the Birmingham businessmen rather than the Cambridge economists who proved to have a better understanding of Britain's post-war economic problems.

It was not, however, on economic issues that the first political crisis of Edward's political career was to arise. In the summer of 1956 Nasser nationalised the Suez Canal. In the autumn Eden invaded Egypt, in collusion with France and Israel. Edward found the combination of bullying, blundering and deceit quite intolerable, and resigned from the government. He discussed the matter deeply with Rab Butler, who tried unsuccessfully to dissuade him from resigning. He did not discuss it much with most of his friends outside the government. History has shown that his resignation was wholly justified, and his judgement wholly correct.

But the price was high. Although he rejoined the government shortly afterwards, when Harold Macmillan had become Prime Minister, the breach with the Conservative Party was never completely mended. After that he was marked as on the left of the party, as perhaps not quite sound, as an idealist rather than a realist. The Conservative Party's main emotions, like Harold Macmillan's, had been those of enthusiasm for the adventure in theory, but disillusion in practice. The party was never quite comfortable with those who had seen the folly of it from the beginning, whether like Edward Boyle they felt that duty called for them to resign, or like Rab Butler felt that the line of duty was to see it through.

After that Edward was seen as someone who would do the idealist jobs, like education, but who was not likely to be a serious contender for the realpolitik jobs like the Exchequer, though the problems of the Treasury still fascinated him. Unfortunately, in political terms, his convictions on educational policy again took him into gradually increasing conflict with his party. He did no more – probably less – to advance the cause of comprehensive schools, or to abolish grammar schools, when he was Minister of Education than Margaret Thatcher was to do under Ted Heath. But his heart was on the comprehensive side of the argument as his heart had been against Suez and the Conservative Party knew it.

The Move Away From Politics

The second resigning issue he confronted was a more personal one. In 1963 he was one of those who wanted Butler to succeed Macmillan as Prime Minister. This time he was persuaded to join the Home administration, I think by Ted Heath, and Iain Macleod and Enoch Powell refused. Again, it made little difference whether or not a minister resigned, if everyone knew already what his feelings were. After 1963, Edward Boyle was already coming to the conclusion that there was no comfortable part for him in Conservative government, that the Conservative Party was moving away from him.

He played his last major political role as a member of Ted Heath's Shadow Cabinet. Ted Heath wanted to keep him, and would have given him office in 1970 – though not the Treasury – and Edward did play a major part in the crisis over race and immigration when Enoch Powell resigned. Yet he was seen by this time as the left wing balance in the Conservative team, and he felt uncomfortable with that. He also felt that the movement of ideas which had led him this far was likely to move him further. When the opportunity to become Vice-Chancellor of Leeds arose he was delighted with it and shed the opportunities and harassments of his political career with little remaining regret.

Looking back now one can see the political and social forces which were destined to push the Conservative Party into its modern Thatcherite stance. With some of these ideas – with the Popper ideal of the open society – Edward Boyle was not out of sympathy. With the values of the Thatcherite Conservative Party he was out of sympathy. Always an intellectual politician, he expounded ideas which increasingly alienated him from the flow of his own party. He reached a point at which the promptings of a strong conscience and a preference for intellectual life finally severed all but residual political links. Oddly enough the undergraduate was closer to what the Conservative Party really felt than was the statesman in his prime.

The parallel is with Gladstone, who was also the most distinguished Tory undergraduate of his generation, who also had an early and successful parliamentary career as a Conservative, who stayed loyal to Peel and who eventually joined and led the Liberals. Rab Butler was Edward Boyle's Peel. But Edward did not have the opening to a new party which saved Gladstone's career. Nor did he have Gladstone's unholy zest for power.

14

The Vice-Chancellor at Work

Christine Challis

One evening late in 1980, as my husband and I chatted with him at his home, Edward Boyle took down a volume and read to us:

> The race of man is as the race of leaves:
> Of leaves, one generation by the wind
> Is scatter'd on the earth, another soon
> In spring's luxuriant verdure bursts to light.
> So with our race; these flourish, those decay.[1]

Given that one of his very first acts on coming to Leeds had been to transform the Lodge by installing numerous bookcases, it was entirely natural that a book should have sprung so readily to hand; and it was entirely natural, too, that exactly the right quotation, elegantly delivered, should have been produced at exactly the right moment to give point to his argument. Within a year the words of the *Iliad* had come true, as of course he had been intimating they would, and as they did so one of the great chapters in the university's history closed.

The news of Edward Boyle's departure from politics to become Vice-Chancellor of the University of Leeds provoked mixed reaction: shock and disappointment among his parliamentary friends on both sides of the House and sheer delight in the university world he was about to enter. In Leeds itself University and City alike revelled at the coup of capturing such a distinguished figure, while further afield fellow Vice-Chancellors were heartened by an appointment which they believed would lift the standing of universities in the public mind and raise morale amongst those working in them. For such a key appointment to produce no controversy is rare indeed in academic life, but in this case 'not even a mouse stirred'. Few Vice-Chancellors can have embarked on a new career with such an exceptional reservoir of goodwill.

Well-versed in the history and development of higher education, Lord Boyle came to Leeds with a genuine understanding of the university's pride in its contribution to the expansion of the 1960s and to the world of learning. Firmly believing that the 'ultimate aim' of universities was the 'pursuit of excellence', he was convinced that, if the universities themselves did not uphold this principle, they could not expect society to do so. To him, it was essential to have departments of high quality, capable of sustaining the highest levels of teaching for able young men and women of university age. He saw clearly that teaching must never lose contact with original research. 'Teaching in the atmosphere of research', as he liked to describe it, was a key concept which he promoted from the beginning, both inside and outside the university.

Although it was accepted without question that after his arrival in Leeds Lord Boyle would continue to play a role in national affairs, it was expected, and readily granted, that the university would become his highest priority. A framework for his role was set partly by the timetable of meetings of Senate, its principal committees, Council and Court; and partly by key public events in the university's annual cycle, notably the honorary degree ceremony with its attendant celebrations, when the Vice-Chancellor, assisted by his sister, Mrs Gold, entertained the Chancellor and her retinue at the Lodge, and the series of degree ceremonies held in July and September. Around these events were fitted appointing committees, briefings, meetings with academics, students, administrators, delegates from overseas and distinguished visitors, visits to departments, public and inaugural lectures, interviews with press and media, and entertainment both within the university and at his home, the Lodge. The week, and most days he was in the university, usually began soon after 9 a.m. with a short period with Maureen Ross who ran the Vice-Chancellor's very busy office and, as he put it, sat 'at the receipt of custom'. On Mondays this first session was followed by his weekly staff meeting with the Pro-Vice-Chancellor, the Registrar and the Bursar, sometimes joined by the Dean of the Faculty of Medicine, and serviced by his personal assistant, Margaret McCreath. At these meetings information was exchanged, the handling of important or sensitive issues discussed, and executive decisions taken on a myriad of matters ranging from the composition of a delegation to China, representation on outside bodies, university hospitality and expenditure from his discretionary funds. Days in the University were exceptionally busy. Rare gaps in the diary were opportunities to attend other committee meetings, slip over to the Library to check a reference or to the Senior Common Room to read the leaders in the principal newspapers.

Naturally enough, his main focal point outside Leeds was London. During the first four months of 1977 and a similar period in 1979 he was in London on no fewer than 29 and 27 days respectively, sometimes two or three times a week. When looking at his diaries one tends to wonder whether he could have contemplated the possibility of the Leeds appointment with such enthusiasm had it not been for the British Rail sleeper service. Additional to the demands of the university and of London were innumerable visits to different parts of the country to speak to educational, academic and professional organisations. Weekends in Leeds either featured meetings in the university, civic and social occasions, or were free of engagements and he was then able to catch up with writing and preparing speeches. This pattern continued throughout his period of office until the last two years when ill-health, particularly during the final year, caused him severely to restrict his external activities. The extent to which Lord Boyle threw himself into the role of Vice-Chancellor and the enthusiasm and commitment he demonstrated meant that, despite his many external commitments, at no time did his senior administrators hear anyone say that he spent too much time away from Leeds.

Lord Boyle saw his role not as the Jarratt-style chief executive of the university but primarily as chairman of the University Senate. Senate's own concept of its importance was reinforced by the emphasis which he placed upon it and by his belief in the importance of debate as a means of achieving consensus in key decisions of vital importance to the university or one of its departments. On his arrival he felt 'rather acutely, that presiding – as a non-academic – over one's first Senate meeting will be *much* more alarming than making one's maiden speech in either House.' This initial anxiety did not show. His effective management of this very large and diverse body reflected careful preparation, thorough understanding of the external environment and its impact on the University, and political judgement. His presentation of often unpalatable truths by judicious use of apt anecdote, ability to handle dissent and to persuade were hallmarks of his chairmanship. Senators, whether experienced former Pro-Vice-Chancellors, heads of departments or relatively junior lecturers had an equal opportunity to be heard. To him it was the content of what was said that was important; the status of the individual only became of relevance when deciding how the issue should be handled. He in turn loved to hear Senate's views and was fascinated by the interplay of debate.

Never shrinking from bringing difficult issues into the open at Senate or the principal committees he chaired on Planning and General Purposes, Lord Boyle sought always to resolve conflict by discussion and rational argument. Administrators sitting on his left often had a good idea of what was in store from the number of non-tipped Balkan Sobranie cigarettes he would lay out in front of him at the start. But while encouraging debate on vital issues, he had an almost unfailing instinct of knowing when it was time for a decision to be reached. Instances abound of his capacity to put forward an acceptable solution at the crucial moment, as when he proposed an increase in support for hardship when the students were up in arms, or £10 000 for an experimental research fund when the original proposal for a permanent and more substantial one had been twice defeated. No one doubted the high priority he accorded to meetings of Senate and these two committees. Other calls on his time had to fit round the Wednesdays when they met. During his last year, despite serious illness, he managed to chair every meeting even if at times the committee had to meet at the hospital or at the Lodge.

These meetings were always preceded by briefings involving the Pro-Vice-Chancellor and his administrative advisers. Issues likely to cause controversy were usually clear and often the precise objections to recommendations known. In some cases it was possible to devise amendments that would not sacrifice the essence of the original proposal; in others it was agreed that the Vice-Chancellor would decide, in the light of discussion, whether to press ahead, refer the recommendation back, set up an *ad hoc* group or propose a compromise solution. The *ad hoc* group was the great Leeds art form of his day and he paid particular attention to the choice of individuals to undertake each special enquiry. Briefings were also opportunities for him to rehearse his approach to a particularly sensitive issue, and to test the reactions of his advisers. After Senate meetings the Vice-Chancellor joined the Registrar and his deputies for sherry and a post mortem, when the impact of individual contributions and the Vice-Chancellor's handling of the proceedings on the outcome of debate were analysed. While welcoming reassurance, he was always ready to accept criticism. Briefings and post mortems were lively sessions, for his ready sense of humour and sharp wit could be sparked off by recollections of pompous contributions or over zealous entreaties from individuals who clearly were taking themselves too seriously.

'Doing what I can to attract really first-rate staff to Leeds' was the other main aspect of his role as Vice-Chancellor that Lord Boyle enjoyed the most. 'Presiding at committees charged with the responsibility of choosing a professor seems to me one of the most important of all my responsibilities,' he said in 1972. He recognised that 'the battle for excellence goes on unceasingly and if one is honest with oneself one has to admit that really first-rate appointments are as rare as essential'; but he never gave up the task. He also chaired committees to appoint the principal administrators, and participated in as many appointing committees for new lecturers as his busy diary permitted. He played a full part in the work of the Senate committee responsible for the appointment and progress of academic staff, including the arduous task of assessing candidates competing for the few senior lectureships available each year.

Well versed in the business of Council and its principal committees on buildings and finance, he took a keen interest in securing funds from the UGC for new buildings and for major alterations. He supported a complicated series of departmental moves which would permit the conversion of space for an expanding department, not because this was the ideal solution but because he was characteristically convinced by a simple general principle that 'the best should not be the enemy of the good'. Less sympathetic to claims for expenditure on the environment, maintenance and minor works, he believed that scholars would accept 'working in a garret' providing the right books were in the library or the departmental grant was sufficient to buy the necessary chemicals. Priority was given to finding money for academic purposes. To exert greater influence on key financial decisions, he decided to set up and chair an Executive Sub-committee to advise the Finance Committee on financial strategy and on the broad distribution of resources between academic and non-academic areas.

With his grasp of finance and awareness of the political scene, he was always swift to recognise turning points in the approach of successive governments to university funding and able to convince his colleagues that changes in the university's policies were necessary. Faced with the prospect of a substantial deficit at the end of the academic year 1974–75 as a consequence of government decisions and rapid inflation, he was clear that, while the university should strive to avoid actions that would be detrimental to its academic standing, it would be irresponsible not to consider ways of effecting reductions in expenditure while – and this was a point he was to make on many subsequent occasions – 'we still retain the freedom of action to plan these economies ourselves'. To harness the support of the community he met all the staff in the Great Hall, announced that the university did not intend to take the easy way out by declaring redundancies, and convinced them of his strategy. His swift response paid off. Public persuasion apart, he led by example, deciding on the retirement of his driver to abandon the university car. Undeterred by the disapproval of his advisers, he was tireless in trying to persuade us to his view. We became used to seeing him at the number 1 bus stop on Headingley Lane and the boyish delight he took in squeezing his ample form into our often unsuitable vehicles. While members of the community aware of this personal sacrifice found it hard to be too vociferous when faced with the loss of a post or amenity, there were personal rewards for the chauffeurs; for many of the most stimulating conversations I had with him were at the Lodge over a glass of Marc de Bourgogne after driving him home. Lord Boyle's financial and political acumen guided the university through other financial difficulties. Sick and only two months from death he steered through the Senate the strategy for dealing with the 10 per cent recurrent economy imposed by the UGC in July 1981, generating admiration for his 'statesmanlike leadership'.

Lord Boyle believed that 'it must be right to associate members of the academic community as closely as possible with administrative actions that affect academic life.' To him it was self-evident that, in a large multi-faculty university of over 10 000 students and over 1000 staff, there must always be some academics in the 80 or more academic departments with the knowledge and skills to help solve whatever problems confronted us. When energy or water had to be conserved, as in 1974 and 1976, or the telephone bill had to be reduced, groups of academics were appointed to advise on how this was to be done, sometimes to the discomfiture of the paid professionals. The upside of this approach was the willingness of the academic community, after the ritual of protest, to accept the often draconian measures which their colleagues proposed or, after experience, politely to ask for aspects of policy to be reviewed, as when senators asked the group on fuel economy to reconsider the level of heating for the next winter after they had shivered through the last.

The Vice-Chancellor's statement to the Court in November each year was an important event serving three main purposes: justifying the use of public funds, reporting key developments to promote the university's image in the outside world, and communicating within the university a sense of where we were and where we were going. Sometimes too they were occasions to seek to influence government thinking on issues of crucial importance to universities. Student numbers, academic and building developments, the university's financial situation and prospects, student maintenance grants and residence, graduate employment, and sometimes academic salaries, were key features of the statement. After the subjects to be covered had been chosen, selected senior colleagues were asked to send briefing material or draft sections to Miss McCreath, who co-ordinated the statement's preparation. He then welded the material into a coherent first draft which was first circulated to the contributors for comment and then discussed at a special meeting, where he displayed on numerous occasions his formidable drafting skills. Earlier and later statements were very much his own. But, even when restricting his contribution to editing material provided, he always added a substantial section which captured the essence of the time or was designed to keep the community in good heart.

Lord Boyle's perception of his role was more in tune with the views attributed to Sir Derman Christopherson who opined that it was not the Vice-Chancellor who produces the steam in a university: that must come from the academic departments. The Vice-Chancellor's job was to turn on the taps. This was not always appreciated by some departments which expected him personally to reverse their declining fortunes or to make the next leap forward. He was never reluctant to give a lead when he judged it necessary, when key university decisions had to be taken about finance, major buildings, expansion of student numbers or the handling of student disturbances, when the long-awaited new Constitution had to be settled, and when a new relationship with the colleges of education in the region had to be formulated. The successful role played by the university in validating degrees of thousands of students studying in the affiliated colleges owes much to his persuasive skills and commitment, involving him in many discussions at the Faculty Boards and the Senate before the crucial decision was taken.

To Lord Boyle a vital part of his task was to facilitate the fulfilment of the constructive aspirations and ideals of members of the university. Listening to staff at meetings or in informal discussions, visiting departments to talk to staff and students, participating in seminars, lunching regularly in the Senior Common Room, where his habit of joining different groups was greatly appreciated, attending some of the Left Lunch Club meetings and other staff events, meant that he was in touch with current thinking. When heads of department came to see him with problems or complaints he invariably liked one of his administrative advisers to be present to point out difficulties in what might be proposed, or to discuss ways forward. He always expected to be properly briefed. He did not subscribe to the philosophy that the Vice-Chancellor's office should be completely open to all and sundry and had a firm sense of when it was appropriate for staff to see him and when it was right that, certainly in the first instance, they should talk to their head of department or see the Registrar. Instances abound of assistance given to colleagues with drafts for books or articles on subjects familiar to him, on draft presentation addresses for honorary degrees, or advice on career development. On seeing a good review of a colleague's book or hearing praise from an outside source, it was not uncommon for him to convey this in conversation or by personal letter. To distinguished colleagues moving elsewhere he was gracious, recognising the university's loss, but concerned that individuals should discover a working environment and life-style which would encourage the fullest expression of their talents.

An invigorating force in the university's intellectual life, he had a remarkable gift of getting to the heart of subjects as diverse as late nineteenth century music, economics and linguistic philosophy. Few Vice-Chancellors can have inspired one of their retiring professors to express appreciation in the form of an elegantly phrased Latin ode. His incredible memory and vast erudition were evident when presiding over public and inaugural lectures. A few key points jotted down on small cards during the lecture were sufficient prompts for an eloquent performance. On countless occasions his audience was grateful for his capacity to distil the essence of an often complex lecture whether in a medical, science or arts discipline and admired his ability to assess its significance in a wider context. The dinner parties which followed in the university were sometimes a trial for wives or guests of lecturers who were not always ready to converse about the subject of the lecture, the wider concerns of the discipline, music or important issues of the day. Since he was a practised and generous host, a dinner party at the Lodge, always accompanied by stimulating conversation, was an experience not to be missed, and was something frequently enjoyed by retiring professors and their wives, academics and senior administrative colleagues.

From the outset Lord Boyle recognised that the contribution of Leeds and other civic universities to education and society had not always been adequately appreciated in Westminster and Whitehall, and his determination to try to remedy this was a thread running through his entire period of office. Soon after he arrived he suggested to Lord Whitelaw that MPs might 'spend their spare time far more profitably paying visits to universities like Leeds and seeing for themselves the really magnificent work (teaching as well as research) which is being carried on in departments . . . than rough-housing with a minority of dissident students' elsewhere. Lord Whitelaw, who assured him that he would take up this point with the new chairman of the Science and Technology Select Committee, was later to accept an invitation to Leeds. Learning in 1978 that Sir Anthony Rawlinson was keen 'to get out of the Treasury building a fair amount and develop at least some superficial direct acquaintanceship with institutions and people with whose expenditure programmes the Treasury is concerned,' Lord Boyle swiftly arranged a small dinner party at the Lodge. Politicians, including Harold Macmillan, Edward Heath and Richard Crossman, and distinguished men and women of public affairs, were invited to visit the university and often stayed overnight at the Lodge.

To successive presidents of the students' Union Lord Boyle was an enlightened Vice-Chancellor who, as one put it, when 'dealing with difficult students and their problems . . . could turn a situation of possible conflict into one of co-operation.' He ensured that within the university proper attention was paid to their legitimate needs for an adequate supply of places in halls of residence and flats at prices that they could afford, for adequate recreational and union facilities, and outside campaigned for improvements in their maintenance grants. Inevitably student occupations took place from time to time about national or internal issues, but he never over-reacted, recognising that this was the fashionable form of protest and needed handling with calm and sensitivity. He never made the mistake of restricting his informal contacts with students to those who played important roles in the Union or were elected students on university committees, sometimes dropping into the student refectory for his 'plate of chips', dining in halls, or visiting departments. Called upon to act as referee by those keenly interested in a career in the civil service, he would only act after careful study of the file and a personal interview. Always ready to help individual students who were studying educational or political issues with which he had been involved, he would provide information, comment on their work or put them in touch with others who could assist. Keenly interested in the educational progress of students, he participated actively in the annual meetings of the Faculty Boards dealing with examination results. Students who failed their examinations or were referred could appeal to him and he took these cases extremely seriously. On one occasion he and the Deputy Registrar, James Walsh, journeyed over a hundred miles to see the parents of a boy who had failed his degree examinations to explain that universities were about ability and accomplishment, and their son, though able, had failed to accomplish.

To Lord Boyle the two departments of the administration under the Registrar and the Bursar were like departments in the civil service. He expected papers to be prepared in good time for meetings, and advice presented in the form normally offered to ministers. He was always prepared to listen and, when not minded to accept advice, always ready to explain why. He had little patience with long-winded explanations or with niggling criticisms of detailed aspects of decisions; colleagues soon learned to focus succinctly on the essence of the problem, on salient points of information and on constructive solutions. The relationship between the Vice-Chancellor and the three successive Registrars of the university, who led the academic administration, was good, as it needs to be. But there can be no doubt of the particularly close relationship between Lord Boyle and Dr James MacGregor, who served the university as Registrar for eight of the Vice-Chancellor's 11 years in office. Apart from the innumerable committees and briefings when the Registrar was present to give information or advice, the Vice-Chancellor often popped into his office to raise a specific query or problem, and on many evenings they discussed problems, ideas and experiences relating to university affairs over a glass of sherry in the Registrar's room. He had the gift of making his senior officers feel that they played an important role in the university's affairs, and they in turn responded with loyalty and dedication. As Bursar Ray Head once said, 'He could make you feel like a king.' I remember being enormously flattered on one occasion when, trying to convey my role as the Deputy Secretary to a puzzled visitor from Whitehall, he likened it to being Secretary of the Cabinet.

While Lord Boyle could not be described as a Town and Gown Vice-Chancellor, he gave full support to those within the university who were concerned to improve links with the community, encouraging the open days when the university welcomed the general public, first in 1974 and then in their thousands in 1977 and 1980. He maintained contacts with a number of the resident senior figures in the city and region, including the Director of Leeds Polytechnic, participated in special civic occasions and welcomed the Lord and Lady Mayoress to the university – on one occasion pleasing the Lord Mayor enormously by sending a record of one of his favourite pieces of music which they had discussed during his visit. He expected the Bursar to form links with the city's business community, and academics to develop the industrial and commercial contacts which would enrich their work.

It was inevitable that a man of such distinction and breadth should receive offers to head other academic institutions. Whereas in his early days he might have contemplated life in due course as master of an Oxford or Cambridge college, as time went on he made it quite clear that he enjoyed being Vice-Chancellor of the university of Leeds, which had become his home, and it was there he intended to remain. Writing to a close friend towards the end of his life, he wished that he could be remembered for his love of music as something that 'means more to me in life than anything save working for the good of this university or else the company of my family amd most immediate friends.' His tenacity of purpose and determination to husband his limited physical resources 'for as long as is humanly possible' to continue his service to the university was legendary. To me he was a truly renaissance man and a distinguished Vice-Chancellor. He commanded respect and admiration, and the affection of those of us who were fortunate enough to benefit from his support, his encouragement and, above all, his wise counsel.

Note

1. From the *Iliad*, Book VI, pub. 1864. trans. Edward Stanley, 14th Earl of Derby, 1799–1869, Prime Minister, scholar and racehorse owner.

15

The Vice-Chancellor and Student Unrest

Sue Slipman

I did not know him well; nevertheless I learnt a valuable, if embarrassing, lesson from Lord Boyle. It was learnt during my days at Leeds University when I had 'masterminded' a student occupation. Organised with military precision, all went according to plan until the University's administration building was occupied. From that point on any semblance of reasonable control was lost. It dawned on me slowly that I had just done something very stupid. This perception was reinforced when I saw the grand piano being taken out of the goods lift and witnessed the first Maoist wall poster go up. The poster had a very un-Maoist, expletive – deleted word poem upon it, and the local anarchist group took up station on the piano. The 'sound system' was set up to allow anyone who felt inclined to express themselves at any stage of the day or night to do so. With sinking heart I tried to organise various committees to keep the proceedings within bounds. I was told there was no need for security as we would feel the need if it arose and spontaneously rise to protect each other. My worry was the portability of the University's property rather than the citizens of the new free state I had helped to found.

Over the next 24 hours I saw the short-term, orderly demonstration I had organised slip through my fingers and become a mad festival for every weirdo who could possibly crawl out of the woodwork. For the first day I sat bemused and appalled at what I had unwittingly unleashed upon the world. On the second day I started to think about how I could undo it. It took a further six days to accomplish this. It was my first step in becoming a 'betrayer' of causes 'revolutionary'.

On the third night Lord Boyle paid us a visit. As Vice-Chancellor of the university he had every reason to be worried about the status and standing of the university. I never knew if what happened next was clever design on his part or naive accident. The occupation took place in 1974, during the miners' strike and power cuts. He was concerned about lights blazing in the university all night at a time when everyone else in Leeds was conserving power. He came into the occupation just to check that no real harm was being done to the building. I had only vaguely seen him in the distance, or in bad press photographs, and at first did not recognise him. I was not expecting to see the Vice-Chancellor late at night going boldly into territory that was beginning to make me feel distinctly uncomfortable. My first thought on seeing him was finally to admit my so far unverified fear that those camped out in his office might have done unspeakable things on the floor, as well as phoning their relatives in Australia, and to hope that he would not decide to visit the site of their misdeeds.

Lord Boyle walked around talking to a number of individuals in a charming manner. Finally he asked to see me: I had to come out of hiding and accept my responsibility. He asked me if there was any way he could address the occupation force. Fearing the worst I asked for a meeting to be 'assembled'. I had no idea what he wanted to say, but I had little doubt about the reaction he was about to witness. As it was late at night the troops were a little worse for wear and brown ale. They gathered slowly from every corner of the building. The mad saxophonist who had been blowing 'sounds' down the sophisticated PA system for days and nights laid down his instrument. The revolutionary cells came out of their anti-capitalist huddles, and as bad luck would have it the revellers had just returned from the pub. The small trickle had grown to 50 or 60; nearly all inebriated and with the fire of the revolution in their bellies, or the red sun of Mao in their hearts.

Lord Boyle stood before the microphone and very gently told the gathering that he was worried about the university's reputation and that he had a request to make; would those assembled agree to turning some of the lights off, please? It was a strange request to make in the circumstances – either calculated to inflame, or a brave attempt to confront the crowd. His manner was not inflammatory, but the timing of the visit was. The response was predictable. A drunken Maoist staggered out of the crowd, unceremoniously but without violence shoved Lord Boyle from his pitch and made an impassioned plea to this ragged trousered army.

'Comrades,' he said, swaying slightly. I winced, fearing the worst. 'Comrades. In solidarity with the miners I propose the motion that we turn every light in the building on.'

'Yeah!' roared back the mob, and having decided by acclaim they rushed out leaving Lord Boyle and myself facing one another, in a total tongue-tied silence.

'I'm very sorry,' I said, somewhat inadequately.

'Yes,' he replied.

Thankfully he left soon after. I did not die of shame, but the red hot flush of it returned every time I thought of that moment for many years. After Lord Boyle's visit I determined to get us out of there immediately. It took a further two and a half days. They seemed a lifetime and success, when it came, had little to do with either my courage in braving the mob and their derision or my eloquent exposition of the case to get the hell out of this mess. It was the boredom factor that gradually wore down the grip of the Maoists and anarchists on the proceedings. First the few 'ordinary' students caught up in the mayhem crept away under cover of darkness. Then the activists drifted off one by one to follow more enticing revolutionary paths. Finally the saxophonist took the reed out of his instrument and packed up. It was clear that the jam session was over. It was time to put the lid down on the grand piano, clear up the mess and solve the mysterious disappearance of (if I remember rightly) 50 golf balls from electric typewriters. The students' Union was presented with a bill for these. I have often wondered if it was ever paid.

The postscript to the story is the real punchline. I met Lord Boyle on only one other occasion. He was Chair of the Committee of Vice-Chancellors and Principals of Universities. I was President of NUS. My team were appearing before a sub-committee of the CVCP to put the case on student grants. I was dreading it. How could I face this man and pretend to be a grown-up after the last occasion of our meeting? Still, I had no choice. I did not tell my accompanying team the story of my previous encounter with Edward Boyle. I thought they might not understand. Besides they were meant to respect me.

As we entered the room and sat down he grinned at me. It was a friendly, conspiratorial smile. 'Ah, Ms Slipman,' he said, 'the last time we met you were otherwise engaged ' or did he say 'occupied'? He also had the grace to take me seriously in the meeting and I would swear that he never blew my cover. He was an educationalist who took the long view of human development, and who numbered an extraordinary tolerance amongst his virtues.

16

The Vice-Chancellor in Office

William Walsh

Sir Roger Stevens announced in 1968 that he would resign as Vice-Chancellor a year before the formal date of his retirement. The latter half of his period of office had been scarred by the political posturing, the demos and sit-ins of the leaders of the students' Union. The beginning of Lord Boyle's time as Vice-Chancellor was similarly disturbed by this detritus of the 1960s. But whereas Sir Roger Stevens had been deeply upset by it, Lord Boyle dealt with it with a singular blend of Franciscan charity and inner lack of stress, opening the doors of his office to the invading sitters and then negotiating their leaders into the ground: evidence, if it were needed, of the superiority of a real politician to a diplomat, however skilled, when it is a question of managing a turmoil or a mob.

The name of Edward Boyle as a possible VC was first mentioned – at least to me – by Sir Ronald Tunbridge, then the Professor of Medicine, who had been concerned with the founding of medical schools in the new British Commonwealth and who had connections with members of both political parties. He was also a shrewd judge in such matters. Edward Boyle's standing in the world of education was, of course, extremely high. His knowledge, likeability and openness were acknowledged on both sides of the political divide. (On the other hand I noticed when speaking at the Coningsby Club at the House of Commons that his educational reputation was not universal among younger Conservative members and journalists.) Sir Roger Stevens, who described himself as a right-wing member of the Labour Party, enthusiastically supported the notion of Edward Boyle as his successor, although he behaved with scrupulous propriety in doing nothing in any way to influence the decision.

I – I was a member of the Committee elected to recommend a name to the Council of the University – knew Sir Edward Boyle in both his roles as educationalist, in government and opposition, and as publisher – he was standing in at this time for Sir Allen Lane, the deceased founder of Penguin. Perhaps I may say that I found little to disagree with him on educational matters except his steadily diminishing enthusiasm for grammar schools, which he regarded as socially divisive but which I, like others who had taught in them, found morally and intellectually justified, institutions which served the nation by opening up society to talent and which did this most effectively in a class-divided system like ours. I used on occasion to dine or lunch with Edward Boyle in London when we discussed politics, educational issues and literary topics. He was, for example, greatly interested in both the work and the personalities of F. R. and Q. D. Leavis. He was a generous host and a charming and responsive guest. He was a touch idiosyncratic about the choice of food and wine. I remember a dinner at the Connaught which consisted of whitebait and salmon accompanied by wine of such dryness that all wetness had been wrung out of it. At the United University Club, on the other hand, where he once pointed out with modest pride the table at which he had written his resignation from the government at the time of Suez, he would insist on the distinctly unassuming Club claret.

It was at one of these meals – at the Junior Carlton as I remember – that we discussed the possibility of Boyle's coming to Leeds. At least that is what I thought we would be discussing. But it rapidly became clear that the fundamental part of the decision had been taken already – namely the decision to leave politics and take a radically new direction in life. None of the persuasive arguments carefully prepared and organised were needed or uttered. Indeed I had to warn him that in my view the hardest obstacle to overcome would be my colleagues' disbelief that a national figure and eminent politician would consent to come to Leeds to take on a new and troublesome job. In that case, it was suggested, perhaps I could put some of the following points to the Committee. The three or four greatest offices of state were no longer open to him – should it turn out, as then seemed highly unlikely, that the Conservatives were returned at the next election. In any case the nature of his own constituency was changing irresistibly. At the same time he was, while comfortable with his own Conservative philosophy, increasingly uneasy with the temper of the new thought and character of the party. He knew Leeds well, both the town and the University. He would be happy to sell his Sussex house and move permanently to Leeds. His sister Ann Gold would help him with the entertainment which is one of the Vice-Chancellor's heavier duties. And he would commit himself absolutely to the job and to the University. In fact in intellect, character and willingness to devote himself to the post he seemed to be the ideal candidate.

And thus indeed he was to appear to the large majority of the committee. (One or two inevitably, were so politically partial as to be unable to tolerate any Conservative, even one as liberal and attractive as Edward Boyle.) In the event the decision to recommend Edward Boyle was one of the most discerning decisions such a body has ever made. Lord Morris and Lord Boyle became the great Vice-Chancellors of the modern University of Leeds. The former turned an efficient local College into a national and international university; he changed its structures; he inaugurated a new constitution and added distinction to its faculty and increased immensely its plant, facilities and student numbers. If Lord Morris was a creator, Lord Boyle was a conciliator. He responded to the idea of an institution. He loved the combination of life and formality, flow and pattern which characterise the living institution. He was deeply engaged with it at Eton, at Oxford, the House of Commons, and at Leeds. An institution, a social and historical order, complex but coherent, was the setting in which Edward Boyle's personality blossomed. It gave him support, stimulation, purpose. On his side he had the gift, in part instinctive, in part cultivated, to infuse the institution with something of his own nature and to modulate it to some degree to fit his own character. It was by no means wholly dependent on his being present so much, for long hours during the day and evening, term and vacation, although it must have had something to do with it.

But more significant was his possession of a *persona* and a presence. His height, his massive figure, ruddy complexion and shambling gait endowed him with a recognisable and dramatic individuality. He *was* his own image. In the middle years of his tenure at Leeds, he used public transport instead of a chauffeur and a university car, and each journey to the university became a personal announcement, even a political statement, and in those days one much welcomed by students. (There is a story or legend at Leeds that he once took his friend Edward Heath to the university by bus, police cars falling in in front and behind the bus in a solemn and unusual procession.) He would regularly and without fuss slip into the students' refectory and talk to his neighbours with genuine interest. Since anyone could discern that he was essentially a private, shy man, his unassuming friendliness made an indelible impression.

Presence of this kind, both a physical and moral quality, is a most valuable qualification for the head of any institution, and especially a university with its vast population of impressionable young adults. It enables the system to be touched by a human and humane nature and sensibility: an immensely important effect in an institution like a university which cannot but be saddled with all those properties making for distance and impersonality – the bureaucracy, the elaborate hierarchy, the cat's-cradle of committees, the remote cloudiness of official language. Over all this Edward Boyle presided with quick intelligence and supple style, infusing it with a measure of his own generosity of spirit.

The Vice-Chancellor of a great university is the head of an immense and complicated enterprise. He may be tempted to think of himself as its director, even as its managing director. Edward Boyle, on the contrary, took seriously the idea of the University as a self-governing community, a concept that the trade-unionisation of university staff leaves increasingly debilitated. His belief entailed the willing and active attendance at innumerable committees, boards, faculties, Senate and Council, even departmental meetings. (I know in his first year or two he visited at length every single department and school in the University.) It all gave him an intimate knowledge both of the scope and the detail of university affairs, and since he had a memory from which impressions appeared never to fade, he could place the most evanescent of matters in its immediate context and historical setting. Most things at Leeds, certainly every important issue, were decided in such bodies after discussion and argument and Edward Boyle's parliamentary experience and dialectical habit of mind made him a master of this form of decision-making debate. He possessed a fine sense of timing and an intuitive gift of entering the discussion at a decisive moment to make a critical contribution at a significant juncture. It was seldom, therefore, that his view did not prevail. His colleagues were not bruised by this because he was invariably generous to those who disagreed with him. Indeed he was sometimes a degree too generous, being apt to concede a corner to the principle the integrity of which he had just convincingly defended. This was most often the case in his dealings with students for whom he always had a strong predisposition. No Vice-Chancellor was ever closer to students than this former Conservative member of the Cabinet.

If the members of the University, both academic and administrative, responded to Edward Boyle with appreciation and in due course with affection, it was because they were aware in him of qualities of mind and character of a truly distinguished kind.

Edward Boyle was not in a formal or explicit sense a religious man, although he had in his youth given serious consideration to this form of human experience. One had, nevertheless, in communicating with him a sense of something perpetually fine going on. Without any conventional sign or practice of religion, all that he did had, as Henry James said of his father, 'reference to an order of goodness and power greater than any this world by itself can show, which we understand as the religious spirit.' Nor could anyone who had so profound and sensitive a relation with the pure and paradisal art of music be held not to have enjoyed a rich spiritual life. I am reminded of Bunyan who felt that the spiritual life, as Leavis reminded us, implied no stern or morose austerity and that a preoccupation with grace entailed no indifference to the graces of life. Intense spirituality in Bunyan included many joys, the joy of society and family, the joy of children eating their bread well spread with honey, above all the joy of song and music. I can hear the Pilgrim's marvellous chiming cry as he contemplates Christiana with her viola, Mercy with her flute, Prudence with her spinet. 'Wonderful,' Bunyan cried, 'wonderful. Music in the house, music in the heart, and music also in heaven.' Edward Boyle had certainly had music in the house and in the heart, and for him music *was* heaven.

Edward Boyle had an intellect which was hospitable to diverse traditions of thought, and a temperament whose sympathies bent this way and that. The authenticity of his response to a host of experiences was matched by the fullness and cogency of his judgement of them. Who that heard them could forget his short, deft verbal essays given after the Inaugural Lectures of new professors, the subjects of which were usually drawn from the remoter reaches of learning. They were small carved cameos of speech, joining understanding to the keenest comment. His sensibility was alerted by a great range of activities, and his knowledge was as apt and grounded in as many. Such a mind, spiritual and materialistic, detached and engaged, was brilliantly qualified to grapple with what is perhaps the most characteristically human and rational of all our actions, namely the relating of fact to value, the confronting of an event with an ideal. If it is, then it would explain why the strongest and most lasting impression Edward Boyle made on one was of sanity – of the coherent, collected, disciplined mind. He did not shrink from, he genuinely welcomed, the disorderly muddle of what in fact occurs.

He had a pragmatic English feeling for the concrete. And as a thinker he was capable of introducing a principle of comprehension into the confusion of events. He had a coherent sense of order. But he was always concerned too with the degree of relevance, the strictness of proportion, between the actual and the ideal so that in all his activity we are aware of a living balance and a braced equilibrium. He was one of those, who, sympathetic to reality, and intelligent about ideals, are also just in relating them. Sanity – the absence of aberration, centrality of judgement and feeling – was sustained and cumulative in his life and work. It was present in innumerable touches, massively there in the total effect of his life and work.

On the one hand, he lovingly appreciated the order and grace of man's achievement, just as he knew what in man is capable of establishing and augmenting it. On the other, he sees man as harassed, torpid, irrational, and brutal. And as in the one category of feeling there is nothing facile, naively optimistic or 'progressive', so in the other there is nothing stark, rigid, or obscurantist. Together these feelings compose an attitude which is at once impassioned and sceptical, appreciative and disenchanted, and which in its calmness, stability and adequacy discloses itself as the product of a mind completely mature, or what is the same thing, of a mind both vital and ordered. Such an attitude to man, 'hopeful without illusion and independent without rebellion', came naturally to one with so keen a sense of fact, so sure a grasp of relevant principle, such mastery in relating one to the other.

As a Vice-Chancellor he was able, out of the deepest conviction, to uphold the noblest purpose of the institution – teaching in the atmosphere of study and research, as he liked to put it – with a vivid sense of the intrinsic value of the individual. 'Respect the individuality of your friend,' said Coleridge, 'it is the religion of the delicate soul.' The spring and vitality of his work as a Vice-Chancellor came from realising in action the living tension between the function of the institution and the value of the person. These human and humane aims he expressed in word and act with urbanity, seriousness and devotion.

Edward Boyle, like Coleridge 'a literary cormorant' and an insomniac, consumed many night hours reading omnivorously in many subjects. He was not a specialist in the university sense – but surely in musical scholarship he was that and more – he was a generalist on the grand scale: in history, politics, economics, education, musicology, literature – and cricket! All this reading was constantly and immediately available to him because of the powerful memory I have already referred to. Hence the richness of his talk. Memory was one of the potent elements of his intellectual life which was both organised round it and a direct influence upon it. A conversation with Edward Boyle was not prospective or speculative, prophetic or imaginative but instead packed and textured with an immense knowledge of what had happened, of what was the case and of the cogency of the past. His reading of his own life and of the experience of the past which had formed it provided him not with a body of doctrine but a humane, untechnical and balanced centre of understanding. Memory became for him a means of insight and over the years a rich habit of perception.

In the course of his career Edward Boyle published little. He contributed to *The Politics of Education* (1971) and *The Philosophy of Karl Popper* (1974). He delivered the Richard Feetham Memorial Lecture on Academic Freedom at the University of Witwatersrand in 1965, the Carr-Saunders Memorial Lecture on Race Relations in 1967, the Gregynog Lectures at the University of Wales, Aberystwyth in 1972 and the Mays Memorial Lecture at the University of Birmingham in 1976. None of these productions was especially memorable or at all commensurate with his powers. It seemed that faced with the necessity of composition a numbness or even atrophy of the creative faculty descended upon him. This strange negative effect occurred at the beginning, or rather before the beginning, of his career when he fluffed his degree at Oxford after being considered one of the half-dozen most brilliant people of his generation, till its close when he had to withdraw having accepted the commission to write the Reith Lectures on the development of British political institutions. Both his Oxford degree and the Reith Lectures were examples of things for which he was, in the unprejudiced spectator's eye, supremely well qualified. (A further oddity is that he wrote fresh, individual and elegant personal letters.) His natural talent was for the spoken not the written word. It was in speech in certain contexts and for particular purposes that his personality became engaged, the complex resources of his mind ready to hand, and his true self operative and effective. He had the gift of enlisting the sympathy of an audience, even a suspicious or potentially hostile one, even on subjects like constitutional reorganisation. The reason was that in his case the surface was directly in touch with the depths, because he was so clearly sincere, just and charitable, and because his pattern of speech, his modest similes, even his vocabulary – which could embrace without flinching such examples of current university language as 'interface' – were patently and with genuine effort being used to communicate with precision and objectivity. On happy occasions he could be felicitous without being at all fulsome. He was also an expert in the discussion of money (as an ex-Financial Secretary to the Treasury ought to be) – one of the most common and charged topics in a society heavily dependent on what can be garnered or earned from a not wholly admiring or even well-disposed nation.

I hope I have not made out Edward Boyle to be a solemn secular saint. He certainly was not that. He had an impish sense of fun and a gleeful boyish humour. He appreciated the graces of life: his icons, his Renaissance drawings, his slightly foxed Piranesi engravings, opera, conversation, wine and food. But he was at heart a deeply serious spirit. In attempting to define this side of him I will touch glancingly on just two notes. He was one who wished to preserve rather than to abolish the past, or more accurately to insist on the past as a necessary element of progress. This was joined paradoxically to a strong faith in the future and in particular to the students who were the future. The double impulse is set in a disposition which Gerard Manley Hopkins called 'that chastity of mind which seems to lie at the very heart and be the parent of all other good, the seeing at once what is best, the holding to that, and the not allowing anything else whatever to be heard pleading to the contrary.'[1]

Perhaps I can illustrate the purity and catholicity of Edward Boyle's interests by referring to the affinity he felt with the great Cambridge critic F. R. Leavis, a man utterly different in character from himself, intense where he was inclusive, fierce where he was mellow. Yet they had much in common. Each lived a life of scrupulous morality without the support of religious faith, each believed with Michael Oakeshott, himself a contributor to *Scrutiny*, the Leavis journal, that one of the prime purposes of a university was to keep our cultural inheritance in good repair; and each agreed that the essential means to this end was the embodiment of the highest intellectual and academic values in the staff and their inculcation in the students. Edward Boyle pointed out that *Scrutiny* had never been intended as an exclusively literary review, and indeed it carried pieces, particularly in the early years, on music, philosophy, political science and occasionally on the physical sciences as well.[2] But of all subjects other than literary criticism, it was music – he was the first to notice – which occupied by far the most space, four hundred pages or the equivalent of a whole volume. Edward Boyle speaks in terms of the highest praise of its two music critics, Bruce Pattison and Wilfred Mellers. Pattison's work on musical history and that of Mellers on Fauré, Mahler and on music in America were splendid examples of *Scrutiny*'s best qualities – exploring intelligence, first-hand response and pioneering judgement. Of the musical critics in *Scrutiny* Edward Boyle said: 'They were not exclusive in their attitudes, they wanted to share their insights with others, and they showed that living and creative response to change and development which Dr Leavis cared about so profoundly.' As indeed did Edward Boyle.

Notes

1. Letters to Bridges, ed. C. C. Abbott, London, 1935, pp. 174–5.
2. Commemorative Symposium on F. R. Leavis, University of Belfast, 1979, p. 38.

17

Guiding the Top Salaries Review Body

Jean Orr

The Top Salaries Review Body had an important place in the last decade of Edward Boyle's immensely active life. He devoted a great deal of time to its work and brought to it a wealth of experience. He had no illusions about the nature of the task, perceived its importance clearly and was – and remained throughout – convinced of its value. He was committed to the work by nature, by background and by personal conviction, and he inspired confidence among both those covered by the recommendations and the informed public. He was appointed Chairman by the Prime Minister when the Review Body was first set up in 1971. It was an inspired choice, for few people can have been as well qualified, and willing, to take on the controversial and demanding task. Lord Boyle was interested, he was thorough, and he was persuasive. His dry sense of humour was to stand him (and the Review Body) in good stead in the face of some of the stranger decisions of government that were to come.

The terms of reference were to advise the Prime Minister 'on the remuneration of the Chairmen and members of the Boards of nationalised industries; the higher judiciary; senior civil servants; senior officers of the armed forces and other groups which may be referred to it.'

The field was small numerically but vital to important aspects of national life. The 'other groups' reference turned out to be at least as demanding and sensitive a part of the work as the main task: in practice, it covered Ministers of the Crown and Members of Parliament and, from 1975, the Peers' expenses allowances. The intention was that each of the four groups within the standing terms of reference would be reviewed 'normally every two years', and an assurance was given by government that the recommendations would be implemented unless there were 'clear and compelling reasons' for not doing so.

In practice, the Review Body's title might more appropriately have referred to 'top people'. In 1971, the salaries were 'top' only in the sense that they were the rates paid to the people at the top of four separate hierarchies: they were not, and had never been intended to be, 'top' in amount. This concept is well illustrated by the first remit immediately after appointment, which covered parliamentary pay, allowances and pensions. A Member of Parliament's salary at that time was £3250.

In the parliamentary field, as in the public services covered explicitly in the terms of reference, the concept of independent review was not new. But, typically, reliance had been placed on ad hoc inquiries commissioned only when pressure had become intolerable (as it had again by 1969). The sensitivities of this area are obvious: there is never a 'right' time to increase the pay of MPs, only a 'least objectionable' time (as one Member put it in a debate in the House in 1970). A scheme to provide for regular reviews of Ministers' and MPs' pay had come to nought in 1970 and the new Review Body thus inherited a very hot potato for its first remit in 1971. But it was 'a natural' for the task, led as it was by Lord Boyle. His twenty years of direct experience as an MP and holder of high ministerial office, applied now from outside the immediate parliamentary fray as Vice-Chancellor of Leeds University, lent additional authority and confidence. These were of key importance in tackling the problems involved in getting salaries and allowances onto a realistic modern basis with proper regard both to parliamentary needs and to public acceptability. Critical – sometimes jealous – eyes are inevitably attracted by the spectacle of Parliament voting itself any pay increase, however demonstrably overdue and necessary in the public interest. The recommendations on this occasion were accepted by the government and by Parliament and were implemented virtually in full.[1] The system had got off to a good start.

In the years to July 1980, seven further reports (from four reviews) were to be put forward on aspects of parliamentary remuneration and expenses allowances. Not all of them had such a satisfactory outcome as the first, but each contributed to the development of a consistent approach. The 1975 review covered the whole field of the 1971 Report plus, for the first time, the Peers' expenses allowance – an item which at that time was frequently interpreted wrongly outside Parliament, and to some extent inside, as an 'attendance' allowance. This enlarged the minefield, and it is difficult to think of a more appropriate body to steer the course through it than the Review Body, with its collective knowledge and wide experience. Real difficulties had arisen for many MPs since the 1971 pay recommendations had been accepted: average earnings had risen by some 85 per cent and the cost of living as measured by the retail price index by over 60 per cent. The salary of an MP, though brought up to date four years previously, was now worth less in real terms than it had been over a decade earlier. It would be hard indeed to find another professional group in that position at that time. Moreover, the demands of the job had increased and revaluation was overdue. While not wanting to make financial reward a prime consideration, the Review Body saw it as fundamentally wrong that able men and women should be deterred from standing for Parliament by the inadequacy of the MPs' salary. It was not prepared to fudge this issue. It was equally clear that the allowances – which recognise Members' responsibilities in both constituency and Parliament and the need to provide for themselves facilities and services (such as secretarial assistance) that would normally be provided by an employer – should be brought to a realistic level. The embarrassment that can arise when MPs are seen to vote themselves substantial increases, especially at times of economic difficulty, were well understood, and the system of involving an independent body was designed to take the matter out of the intensely political arena. Above all, there was serious concern at the consequences of continuing to undervalue the demands on those elected to govern the country and the Review Body focused attention on the fact that failure to provide realistic remuneration simply stored up greater difficulties for the future.

The government and the House of Commons accepted that the £8000 salary recommended for MPs in 1975 was appropriate but decided to implement it for pensions purposes only: the amount actually to be paid was reduced to £5,750. One result was that Members had to pay higher pensions contributions out of the lower 'actual' salary. Such is the kind of anomaly that arises when a closely knit package of measures is unpicked selectively, notwithstanding the fact that the Review Body had been at pains to emphasise that the recommendations were designed as a coherent package intended to be treated as such. Only those that affected allowances and facilities were fully implemented: the others were either modified or shelved. Hair shirts were very much in fashion. One glimmer of light was a decision to implement the recommendations on the parliamentary pensions scheme itself.

Inevitably, the next review (1978–79) took place against a background of serious problems: the 1975 salary recommendations had not been implemented and in the succeeding years inflation had continued to eat into the real value of the salaries actually being paid. The Review Body made the point unequivocally.[2] In the event the outcome was rather more satisfactory than in 1975. The recommended levels of salaries were accepted as appropriate for June 1979. Inevitably the increases proposed were large and they were therefore introduced in three stages but at least the deferred payments were to be brought up to date. The other recommendations were accepted in principle but several were significantly modified, the government again taking the view that there were 'clear and compelling reasons' for this course. In the event, the second and third stage increases were restricted. The House accepted the government's proposals.

A key issue throughout the reviews to date had been the question of linking parliamentary pay to some external indicator or salary. Again, the Review Body had a clear view and came down firmly against such an outside link, whether with general pay or price movements or with a particular grade in the Civil Service. Both propositions had been considered and turned down in the first two reviews and the Review Body again maintained in 1978–79 that MPs' pay should be judged on the demands of the job itself, taking account of all the relevant factors, and that Members ought not to be insulated from public discussion of their pay. The various outside link proposals seemed largely designed to duck the problem – common to the top salaries field generally – of unsympathetic publicity and political embarrassment. The key was seen by the Review Body as frequency of review; and biennial review by an independent body was recommended with a full revaluation at alternate reviews. Lord Boyle was himself fully convinced of the rightness of this view. Nobody was more aware that the recommendations were often unpopular with governments, but he saw clearly that the size of the increases was largely a consequence of failure to keep pay at appropriate levels in the 'top' people's structures, including the parliamentary field.

In July 1980 the House accepted a government proposal that a Select Committee should be appointed to examine

> the desirability and possible method of conducting reviews of Members' salaries by an independent body once during the first session of each Parliament and of adjusting salaries during the

period between such reviews by reference to increases in the remuneration of a designated group of outside occupations.

The Select Committee recommended in 1982 that the Review Body should review Members' pay in the fourth year of every Parliament and that provision should be made for updating salaries between reviews. These recommendations come close to the thinking behind the Review Body's thesis on the need for regular and frequent review, reiterated in 1981 (though the method for updating between reviews is another matter) and Lord Boyle would have regarded the development as an important step forward.[3]

Looking back over the decade of the Review Body's involvement in parliamentary remuneration and allowances under Lord Boyle, the conclusion must be that, notwithstanding the occasions on which recommendations were varied, staged or otherwise modified, much was achieved. He had a natural instinct for what Parliament (and the informed public) would wear as regards salaries and allowances and a firm belief in the need to provide salaries that were appropriate to the full demands of the job, taking proper account of its public service nature and unique character. His approach was realistic and pragmatic, laced with a strong sense of justice and 'fair play' – to both recipients and providers of parliamentary remuneration – and recognition of the importance of clear and consistent principles. If those principles were too often set aside for immediate expediency, it remained important that they at least had an avenue of public expression through the Review Body, which could be expected to facilitate a more informed public debate.

The parliamentary field, albeit politically sensitive, was relatively straightforward and self-contained. The remit on the four fields specified in the terms of reference was far more complex and extensive studies were involved.[4] The recommendations formed an interdependent edifice, the coherence of which was seriously damaged when governments felt the need selectively to modify elements of a report. What made someone of Lord Boyle's remarkable qualities and wide-ranging gifts and interests devote so much time and effort to what must often have seemed a thankless and unproductive task? It must have been frustrating to a man of his intellectual calibre and integrity, first to see the product of so much thorough and painstaking work and careful judgement so often 'modified' or even pigeon-holed in the interests of what, on occasion at least, seemed to be short-term political expediency (and this notwithstanding express assurances on acceptance of recommendations barring 'clear and compelling' reasons against); second, to know from experience that the short-term expedients would inevitably spawn long-term problems of the kind that the spurned recommendations had been designed to cure; and third, in the parliamentary field, to encounter repeatedly arguments for the supposed panacea of an outside link for the salary of MPs, notwithstanding the Review Body's closely and consistently argued view that independent and regular review was a much better way of tackling the problems. Lord Boyle was not opposed to an incomes policy but he was firmly against the singling out of groups of public servants for adverse discrimination as regular examples to the rest of the community. He had a keen eye for the long-term effects of such an approach on recruitment and therefore on the quality of future leadership in the different fields.

Why then did he carry on? One explanation – probably the main one – lies in his strong sense of public duty. The field for which 'his' Review Body (for so it was, although he would not have expressed it in that way) was responsible, tended to be unpopular with the public and the press. 'Top' people were too often confused in the public mind with 'rich' people who (it was held) could well afford to be left behind still further in the salaries stakes, without serious damage to them or to the important areas for which they were responsible. Throughout all the frustrations, he was unshaken in his conviction of the essential value and importance of the Review Body's function in a parliamentary democracy. Moreover, he *liked* the job, notwithstanding the frustrations, and he clearly liked and enjoyed the company of his colleagues and revelled in the opportunities for wide-ranging discussions, particularly in the oral evidence sessions, of all aspects of the problems involved. He seemed also to welcome the opportunities that the work provided to keep in touch with 'the centre' (both Ministers and senior civil servants) and otherwise to take the pulse of opinion surrounding the work. Contrary to some misconceptions, the Review Body was never in the vanguard in any 'pay round' – its operations were without exception rearguard operations designed to restore the people within its terms of reference to an appropriate place within the general structure of pay in the country as a whole, taking account of all facets of the jobs. In spite of setbacks as regards the fate of some of the recommendations, Lord Boyle never seriously contemplated resignation: he preferred to continue the battle from the position of influence and more than once he convinced understandably cross colleagues of the preferability of staying on in order to carry the work forward for the sake of the longer term. He inspired great loyalty and much affection. The demands on the time of all members of the Review Body were very substantial, but heaviest on the Chairman, particularly in the extensive sessions of oral evidence that were part of each major review. These sessions were particularly fruitful: Lord Boyle certainly put into practice his belief in the importance of thoroughness. His encyclopaedic knowledge of the field impressed all who came into contact with him. His colleagues recall his gift for the illuminating and memorable turn of phrase which, combined with his cheerful sense of humour, leavened the lump of solemn business and made it all such fun. His skill in drawing out 'witnesses' and getting to the root of the problem was legendary, as was the unfailing good humour which underlay his ability to defuse pomposity without giving offence. As regards this field of activity which was clearly dear to him, it is difficult to improve upon the judgement of the obituary notice in *The Times* on 1 October 1981:

> His top salaries work brought to the fore Boyle's developed sense of natural justice. He believed that figures alone were not enough: a degree of judgement was necessary on intangibles like job satisfaction and public prestige. His sympathy for the value of public service and those who worked in it, demonstrated in his commitment to the Fulton Committee on the Civil Service, was of great value to him in reporting on top salaries and made a firm impression on those working alongside him. However strident the criticism of public servants in the community at large, Boyle never lost sight of their true worth to the nation.

Many in the public services and beyond will not lose sight of his true worth or of the lasting value of the work done under his leadership in the Review Body's first ten years. Those who worked with him remember the experience vividly and with a lively sense of privilege.

Notes

1. The increases for Ministers were staged.
2. Report No. 12, paragraphs 78 and 79.
3. This has since been overtaken by a resolution of the House of July 1987, under which the salary of MPs is calculated as a percentage of

the maximum of the basic salary scale of a grade 6 civil servant. This link has to be confirmed within three months of every new Parliament by affirmative resolution of the House.

4. A fuller account of the activities of the TSRB 1970–81, which includes the work done on the the four groups specified in the terms of reference, has been deposited with Edward Boyle's papers at the Brotherton Library, Leeds University.

18

Edward as Musician
Alexander Goehr

'Tovey, if I may quote him just once again, says that the ending [of the Adagio of Brahms' 2nd Sextet] reminds him of "a sky in which all clouds are resting on the horizon and dazzlingly white"; I can only say that, for me, that image doesn't quite do justice to the patch of colour in the very last bars when a D natural on the first viola is twice contradicted by a D sharp on the second. Incidentally, the second cello, who has if it must be admitted a dullish time during much of the sextet, fully makes up for it in this adagio.'

Unfair perhaps to write out now what has been crossed out in the manuscript, but irresistible to me as a snapshot revealing the characteristics of the man! First we have a reference to authority, to Donald Francis Tovey, Reid Professor at the University of Edinburgh, who more than anyone else set the tone and preoccupations of enlightened musical thinking, both of professionals and amateurs in his own times. 'Just once again', says Edward, but only to revise what is after all no more than a metaphor, to get it quite right, to justify the subjective and evocative image with a specific and concrete observation of detail. And then, heralded by the ubiquitous, 'incidentally', he joins on an acute observation of his own.

I dwell lovingly, if a bit pedantically, on such trivial details because Edward Boyle had the speechmaker's gift of writing very much as he spoke, and speaking straightforwardly as he thought and was. There is a striking similarity between his language and utterance and his mind. As he was a reticent, even shy, man, and as it would be an impertinence for me to claim an intimate understanding of how he was on the basis of the regrettably too few years that I knew him, and above all because he himself, if he would at all have wished anyone to write about him, would have been the first to observe any false tone, it seems appropriate to try to portray him through the things that concerned him and, as far as possible, according to the values he held dear to himself.

There were always those, in the University and in Leeds, who sought to know Edward Boyle in a more intimate and revealing way than may have been possible. Such people, though well aware of his personal warmth and consideration in his dealings with those around him, may nevertheless have felt a certain impersonality in such dealings. Although a man equipped with a phenomenal memory will hardly have been able to avoid a measure of personal reminiscence ('1936 – a remarkably hot summer: on August —, at Lords, Ranji scored a magnificent innings of —'),[1] he seemed primarily to have been concerned with a world of objects outside himself. They were part of a perpetual present, to be appreciated, understood, defined and finally remembered. Houses, gardens, food and wine, fine art, music and literature, to say nothing of the statements of politicians and thinkers, all were arranged in that remarkable storehouse of his memory, ready to be brought out and re-examined at any moment. He certainly seemed less concerned with abstract ideas or theory, certainly as far as music was concerned. A foray on my part into the higher abstractions would, as often as not, be received in silence, or at best, with a corroborating or by implication critical but always concrete example. The impression of impersonality may be given, when taste and knowledge result from a mulling over of accumulated and carefully observed detail. He did not work by hunch, intuition or the association of disconnected observations bridged by personal feeling. He made no jumps or generalisations. Doing quite the opposite myself (as will be obvious from what I write about him), these characteristics of his often caused me a certain uneasiness in our conversations. On the one hand, without a detailed memory for musical themes, chords and procedures at my disposal, I found myself in a perpetual condition of mendacity, saying that I remembered things that I didn't, because had I said that I did not know that moment in the piece he was referring to, he would probably have regarded it as an unfairness on his part to display superior knowledge. But then again, I had to take care to avoid abstract rodomontade and try to say things in a more concrete and justified manner to retain his interest. When he had nothing to say, he said nothing and the conversation had to start anew. But in this way, he taught me a great deal.

Mention of impersonality and of a concern with detail might suggest little more than a kind of connoisseurship, a polite way of describing the mentality of a stamp-collector. But this would be quite short of the mark. Eliot uses the notion of impersonality in relationship to what he described as 'the responsible man interested in poetry'. (How well that fits Edward!) 'To divert interest from the poet to the poetry is a laudable aim,' Eliot writes (in *Tradition and Individual Talent*, 1917), 'for it would conduce to a juster estimation of actual poetry, good and bad. There are many people who appreciate the expression of sincere emotion in verse, and there is a smaller number of people who can appreciate technical excellence. But very few know when there is an expression of significant emotion, emotion which has its life in the poem and not in the history of the poet. The emotion of art is impersonal.' Edward surely knew this passage and would have agreed with it, though he would not have written it down, if he had thought of it, for to have done so would almost have involved an act of self-observation and generalisation which of itself would qualify the very impersonality described. But like Eliot's 'responsible man', he proceeded from the observation of detail to the recognition of the significant emotion which he believed it encapsulated. The belief that a detail encapsulates an emotion also lies behind Tovey's thinking and stands to some degree at variance with the present-day preoccupation with structure and function. Edward's thinking about music was more than the sum of its parts, despite the fact that he continually expressed himself in terms of the details, preferring technical precision in description and chiselling away to get a metaphor just right. As he never insisted, he left it to his listener to feel his deeper meaning.

Recall of the single, significant detail and the moment at which it occurred almost took on the form of a personal mannerism, and was the thing picked up by his mimics in the Leeds Senate. In a note thanking me for a dinner, he inevitably mentioned one dish which he had particularly enjoyed, and in congratulating an artist on a performance, the sentence beginning, 'I particularly admired . . . ' soon came up. As can be imagined, disagreement or disapproval was always expressed tactfully and hedged around with qualifications. But if somebody said something that Edward found ridiculous, he would say, 'That would never have occurred to me.'

Nobody who was present at the degree-giving ceremony at the Royal Northern College of Music in 1981 can possibly forget his speech on behalf of the honorary graduands. Thin and emaciated now, his firm voice choking with emotion, he said, 'I have no right under any accepted definition of the word to call myself a musician. But I would just make one claim; I do wonder whether anyone outside the world of professional music can ever have loved this art more than I have done, and when I listened recently to the new von Karajan recording of *The Magic Flute*, when I listened to the first side of the Second Act, from the March of the Priests to the end of Sarastro's second aria, I felt a quite renewed and special sense of the beauty and nobility of the sound, even on a recording of operatic spectacle, and a conviction that here is composition which represents the human imagination at its highest possible pitch. And I felt that to have known and loved music of this transcendent quality has in itself, quite apart from anything else, made life seem to have been infinitely worth living.'

As appears to have been the case with so many musicians and 'those who feel they have no right to call themselves musicians', Edward may initially have derived his love of music from his mother whom, in another part of the same speech, he described as an 'amateur 'cellist of some accomplishment', who delighted specially in playing chamber music. Ann Gold believes that it was at his Prep School at Abinger Hill, which he attended from 1933 to 1936, that 'Edward discovered his interest in music, and then found that his mother shared the interest.' In conversation, he frequently mentioned his mother and quoted her opinions, which in their style and penetration clearly affected his own. He gives a picture of her 'in her musical home' in the Foreword he provided for Joseph MacLeod's study of the Sisters d'Aranyi, who had been close musical friends of the family from the time when his father shared chambers with Alexander Fachiri in the Temple. Lady Boyle had trained in Dresden immediately before the First World War and, as her son writes, 'one of the proudest and happiest moments in her life occurred when Adila Fachiri invited her to play in the small string orchestra which accompanied her and Jelly d'Aranyi at the Haslemere Festival.' It was in the Boyle house that Adila first came downstairs and announced, 'Schumann has come to us,' referring to the rediscovery of the Schumann Violin Concerto. 'It did not prove a fortunate visitation,' continued Edward, and then with his inevitable desire to be quite just, 'but, as a music-lover, I cannot regret the disinterring of this Concerto, if only for the sake of the opening bars of the slow movement'!

I never heard Edward play a note on the piano, nor indeed have I seen a note of music written in his hand. No musical manuscript is contained in the papers deposited in the Brotherton Library in Leeds. But his detailed knowledge not only of scores, but of compositional techniques suggest that he was well able to represent scores at the keyboard for his own ends. One Christmas, I gave him a copy of André Gedalge's classic and monumental 'Traité de la Fugue'. (Not everyone would wish to receive this for Christmas!) Thereafter we frequently discussed details of fugal technique and I remember him saying that he was capable of writing an adequate, if entirely unoriginal, fugue. I formed the impression that he had, from time to time, made the attempt to compose movements of various kinds, but doubtless these found their way to the wastepaper basket. Nobody who has not tried for himself could have developed his intense admiration for the fact of creativity; or, conversely, nobody who took such an intense interest in the means of composition, would not at some point have put pencil to paper. His last school reports, written by Henry Ley, who was to be a lasting influence upon him and whose opinions he regularly quoted, point to 'considerable ability' in his command of musical theory. 'How far he hears what he writes without going to the keyboard, I am not prepared to say.' In the following report, his last term before leaving Eton: 'He shows promise and originality. I hope he will write a minuet and trio for string quartet during the holidays. He has a real sense of style and economy of notes.' Sir Thomas Armstrong remembers that he was 'a frequent presence with me in the organ-loft at Christ Church . . . He often brought with him chants and hymn-tunes that he had composed, and themes or fugue-subjects on which he would ask me to extemporise,' but 'I don't remember him ever wanting to play the instrument himself.'

Modern developments in communication have made music available to a measure which could hardly have been imagined fifty years ago. But those who grow up now and who can hear so much are not always encouraged to learn to listen with the whole attention and in that way acquire the habit of aural parsing. Though the ability to identify and, as it were, translate back into notation is not necessarily the *sine qua non* of aesthetic experience, it does provide a fund of precisely observed moments which may later be recalled and made to serve as a basis for comparison of compositions and their performances. To put it less pessimistically, there is now, as there could not have been earlier on, a new and additional public for serious classical music, who come to it innocently, without technical foreknowledge. The fact of this new public swelling the ranks of music lovers, and their consequently different modes of perception, depending as they do on spontaneous and intuitive feelings, make what was once understood as listening seem exceptional and the prerogative of the professional. In this sense, Edward certainly was a 'musician'. Over the years he had developed his ear; his sense of pitch, if not absolute, was very near it. The combination of total and critical attention combined I suspect with the regular habit of doing his homework made it possible for him, in the traditional sense, to 'compare and contrast' compositions and their performances. He was able to summon up instantly a whole repertoire of past performances of most of the standard concerti, symphonies and quartets. This ability made him the ideal choice for the crucial position of chairman of the jury at the Leeds Piano Competition, where he surely had the time of his life, as well as winning the unanimous respect and affection of the great pianists and teachers who came to Leeds and who, *pace* Fanny Waterman, are not generally associated with the ability to agree, recognise each other's strong points or even be civil to each other. But this aspect of his musical life is dealt with elsewhere, and I only want to record the pleasure he took in the successive competitions right up to his last days, and the friendships he made there, all of which contributed to the great admiration and personal affection he felt for Fanny Waterman.

The same qualities of musicianship lend a particular flavour to the relatively few studies of works and composers he managed to complete. Those who knew him find it extraordinary, not that he wrote so little, but that in his active life and with such a variety of interests and responsibilities he managed any at all. It is hard to know when he did all that he did. Maybe, in Pierre Boulez' apt phrase, 'he slept fast'.

Edward probably felt most at home writing programme notes for concerts. For his fiftieth birthday he invited his friends to a party at the Hyde Park Hotel where, extraordinary as it may sound, he had once attended classes in ballroom dancing. There was no ballroom dancing on this occasion; instead, and probably preferable to his guests, he offered a recital of *lieder* by Elisabeth Schwarzkopf and Gerald Moore. I am sure that Edward took the planning of the recital very seriously and had as much influence as he could have had on the content and ordering of the groups of songs. Characteristically he had prepared detailed notes for each group of songs, believing as always that everybody, even at a birthday party, had come to listen seriously and consider each song with full attention. The way he prepared a note tells quite a lot about him. Inevitably there was a résumé of the text, the date and the location of the song in a cycle, if appropriate. There was always the observation of one favourite device or moment clearly described, and more often than not a ranking of the song in relation to comparable songs or settings of the same text by other composers. I always suspected that there must have been a mental connection between his liking for ranking and the way he had experienced policy-making decisions in government or university. In music as in administration he seemed to wish to give the impression, or perhaps he really did believe, that the best song was the one with the best discernible features, as the best decision was the one with the most predictable advantages and the least risks. I once heard Benjamin Britten say a similar thing, that a piece was good because it had good features. I cannot easily understand this; for me, love and value arise out of an overall aesthetic impression into which, but not essentially, I will fit the observed detail. But Edward really enjoyed ranking preference and chronology. He organised his large and ever-growing record collection, or so I believe, according to the date of composition of the principal piece on each record. (I do not understand how this could have worked, and maybe the system was more complicated.) I would not have been surprised if he had ordered the compositions of each composer and performances according to his preferences! Whatever the system, he had no trouble in putting his finger on what he wanted.

In essence, the two lectures upon which he lavished most attention and devoted to the two composers, Brahms and Fauré, were organised on similar principles. As I recall them now, before rereading them in detail, they were ordered collections of interconnected notes on individual movements or songs. As with the programme notes, infinite trouble was lavished on the finding of the *mot juste*, the appropriate metaphor, and where words are involved, the way in which the composer objectified his own understanding of the words. Here again he much admired ranked catalogues, and at the time when he was collecting material for his regrettably unwritten BBC guide to the music of Fauré, he was very excited by the thesis of Professor Françoise Gervais, who listed the principle harmonic usages of Debussy and Fauré, each section of which is little more than a collection of examples rather like a concordance. This Gallic mode of musical analysis suited him perfectly.

It might seem that this is a rather dry, if entirely respectable, way of discussing music. But the effect of the lectures was not at all dry, firstly because of Edward's particular character of speech and secondly because he would qualify and colour his observations with isolated anecdotes which threw new light upon his subjects and often upon himself. Although any form of self-dramatisation was totally foreign to his nature, I could never quite resist a feeling that he identified with the rather inward and unostentatious personalities of Brahms and Fauré, different as they may have been from each other. I suspect this impression resulted from his choice of anecdotes and quotations of their own words and his own approval or disapproval of them. He was particularly fond of a letter from Brahms to Clara Schumann, in which, talking about belief in God, he suggests that 'we', himself and Clara (I'm sure Edward wanted to be joined to the 'we'), 'have in music something better than belief'. I have never found this letter (though I have not looked very hard), I'm sure because I partly wish that Edward had made it up – although I know he never would have done such a thing. When Fauré cruelly reproaches his wife, to whom he seems to have been regularly unfaithful, with the observation that she could have heard 'on one and the same day, praise accorded to the beauty of a father's sculpture and of a husband's musical composition,' and that if her life had turned out sadly, this was because she had vainly wanted to be a 'somebody' on her own account, Edward comments, 'I confess that these words have sometimes made me feel uneasy while preparing this lecture.'

Perhaps one of the reasons why Edward was so successful as Vice-Chancellor at Leeds was because he made everybody feel that they were part of an enterprise or a community. One of the ways he did this was by generously quoting the pearls of wisdom uttered by others and made to sound a bit better and less banal when spoken by him. ('I'm particularly grateful to Professor Goehr for the important observation that most cheese is yellow.') Few were those who did not feel a few inches taller by being singled out in this way. Nor was it only the very grand he quoted. He brought the words of the lowly into the halls of the mighty, and I would not have been surprised if he had quoted a sentiment of his cleaner at the Vice-Chancellors' meetings in London. He made us feel better than we might otherwise have felt we were and perhaps, as a result, we were a bit better.

The same generous paying of respect colours his articles on music. He likes to quote, give credit and gently correct or modify the views of other writers. He gives generous appreciation to writers like Nectoux, Robert Orledge and Norman Suckling who shared his enthusiasm for Fauré, but pokes slight fun at Suckling who had an almost pathological dislike of the Viennese classics and especially Beethoven. 'I don't happen to share Norman Suckling's dislike for middle-period Beethoven,' he writes, 'but one must admit that Suckling *has* a point about what he calls the "tyranny of the leading note" – there were far too many commonplace progressions from dominant to tonic in much 19th century music.'

This to point out 'how beautifully Fauré in the last line of Le Secret (Aux plis de sa robe pâlie) avoids this hackneyed effect. One's always being reminded, when listening to Fauré, of the infinite difference between pedestrian note-spinning and truly distinguished composition'. The effect of his lectures is of continuous dialogue, and this as much as anything else gives them their life. They are spare in style, informal and free of special pleading. One regrets the projects which were not realised.

It would be easy to remember Edward Boyle just as the cultivated and enlightened man that he was. But to do so would fall a bit short of the truth by emphasising what are after all fairly conventional aspects of his background, upbringing and career. Yet there was another, shyly passionate and intense side of his nature, which I refer to with diffidence and an acute sense of the dangers of sentimental distortion. Indeed some of those who knew him might see nothing unconventional about his life except his untimely death: early brilliance and success, member of what we like to call the Establishment, Minister of governments, and at the end, Vice-Chancellor of an important university. But I feel there was a bit more to it, while well aware that what I want to emphasise may merely be the recognition of a reality as opposed to some stereotyped notion I may have had of what a man like Edward Boyle ought to have been. I refer to what only indirectly concerns me here – the development of his political thought or, perhaps more accurately, his beliefs about modern life. Early on in our friendship, I was very surprised by what seemed to be a remarkable divergence between his beliefs and the beliefs one would as an outsider assume to be appropriate to a Tory minister, even one in those far-off days! Aided by alcohol, I asked him about this, and he told me that he had been a Tory for two reasons: the first, because young men of his background who wished to go into politics moved naturally into the Tory Party, and more substantially because while giving nothing to Socialists in his commitment to reform and social justice he believed that more could be done by the coincidence of wise men of goodwill in power than by the application of a theory or dogma. He believed that good government would most likely result from the election of those fittest to govern and could understand why some people might have voted for the Labour Party at several elections since the war. I asked whether he still believed this and he answered that regretfully he did not, because he now (this was the early 1970s) perceived the Tories as ideological and dogmatic. It was difficult to reconcile these fundamental beliefs with his fascination for Marxists and the ideologies of the extreme Left. As I got to know him better I sometimes regretted what my question about his politics revealed of myself. Though quite improper here to speak of myself, I have to acknowledge a special debt to him, for in matters musical as well as political he helped me at least to try to shed an element of unattractive dogmatic authoritarianism and adherence to received ideas, which would previously have seemed to me to represent a refusal to compromise, but was surely not free of false posturing.

But I am not briefed to talk politics. To my eyes, perhaps a bit conventionally, I see Edward as a man born and bred in civilised and privileged circumstances, sensitive and shy and therefore a bit apart and sometimes ill-at-ease with those around him. At the same time he was open and available and above all interested in what everyone had to say. I did not know him as a constituency MP in Handsworth, but in the years in Leeds he seemed to be pursuing some ideal of community and of personal participation within it. His community was classless, caring and inclusive, and it is maybe not too much to suggest that the musical life was one of its models. He saw in the pursuit of music an activity which brought people of different ages, abilities and backgrounds together. He intensely admired creativity at its centre and, I suspect, considered himself not to be creative. He certainly believed in the pursuit of excellence (which is the code name for artistic exclusivity), but just as important were the rudimentary first steps of the young and the consolations brought by simple forms of music-making to the physically and mentally handicapped. He passionately believed in comprehensive education ('As Minister, I never received a letter from the parent of a child in a secondary modern school, regretting the absorption of this type of school into the new system') and the comprehensive culture to which it might lead. He regretted nothing. A connoisseur of fine food and wine, he acquired a Penguin Cookbook for moderately incompetent bachelors and took to preparing his own suppers. He was quite unperturbed by a student occupation of his office (as was the custom in those far-off days) and took his work to a table in the students' Union or the University Library. When the occupation army had withdrawn, they left on the wall of the private toilet, for its proprietor to read, the message: 'Boyle is a bourgeois bastard.' The cleaners came to excise this folk wisdom, but he said, 'You'd better leave it for a bit, it will do me good to think about it once a day.' He delegated authority well, but not where the welfare of a recalcitrant student, mental or physical problems, or financial hardship were involved. These things he saw to himself, and he defended the interests of the poorest individuals as if the survival of the state depended upon them. I always suspected that some of his successes at obtaining assistance for all kinds of people in fact came from his own pocket, but of course I do not know this. The students at Leeds seemed to sense his qualities and that is why they loved him. All who had dealings with him were met with compassion, respect and generosity, as well as the assumption that they loved Fauré and Brahms as much as he did himself. That is why so many of us miss him in our hearts.

Note

1. Editor's note: Edward would have known, of course, that in fact Ranjitsinhji, 1872–1933, ceased to play cricket in England after 1920.

19

Presiding at the Leeds Piano Competition

Fanny Waterman

I first met Edward Boyle in 1965. He had been invited in 1964 when Minister for Education to open the new Assembly Hall of the Leeds Grammar School but by the time the date came round he was out of office, there having been a change of government.

He had noticed in the newspapers that a student of mine, Michael Roll, winner of the first Leeds International Pianoforte Competition, had just performed Mozart's Piano Concerto in E flat K 482 at the Royal Festival Hall and he enquired which cadenza he had played. I replied that he had composed one for himself to which he responded, 'I hope he made good use of the second subject as Mozart does not use it in the development section'. The conversation proceeded as Edward reviewed each of the Mozart Piano Concertos in turn, indicating those to which Mozart himself had written cadenzas, and who had written cadenzas to the rest.

It was an awesome first meeting, initially because of Edward's immediate recall of facts and figures and later because of the conversation which followed about the supremacy of the Mozart Piano Concertos and the various performances both live and on record that we had both experienced. As Mozart is my favourite composer, and I had either taught or performed almost every one of these concertos, the talk flowed enthusiastically but I did not realise then that for the next 16 years, he, Geoffrey (my husband) and myself would discuss and appreciate together so many other musical masterpieces. It was the foundation of a deep friendship which lasted until his death.

Mozart was not his only specially-loved composer. He was particularly fond of the piano music of Fauré and had made a detailed study of it; but apart from the piano, his heart and mind ranged over the whole gamut of music – opera, *lieder* and chamber music as well as orchestral and instrumental. We would continue the conversation

Presiding at the Leeds Piano Competition

as long as possible, occasionally even challenging him on matters of musical fact, but he was as accurate as he was perceptive.

It was in 1970, after he had become Vice-Chancellor of the University of Leeds, that our friendship became really close. We had attended a concert together after which a reception was to be given at a nearby hotel, about five minutes' drive away. We offered him a lift (he never learned to drive as he maintained that there were already far too many bad drivers on the road without him adding to their number). Naturally we discussed the concert with special reference to the performance of the solo pianist, and in those few minutes I realised that Edward's knowledge of music and its performance was not only factual and intellectual but also as sensitive emotionally as that of any professional musician whom I had ever met. He knew the score of the concerto in every detail and his acute listening over many years to numerous performances of the piano literature made him an ideal choice for the chairmanship of the jury for the next Leeds International Pianoforte Competition in 1972. My hasty invitation during that short car journey received a non-committal reply but with it a promise that the offer would be very carefully considered. He later told me that he was reticent about accepting my invitation at once as he realised that he would be succeeding Sir Arthur Bliss, Master of the Queen's Musick, the first chairman, and his successor, Sir William Glock, at that time Controller of Music, BBC. Within a few days a reply, by hand (it was at the time of a postal strike), came to the home of Marion Thorpe, my co-founder, where I was staying at the time. It was in the affirmative.

It was in this capacity that we got to know Edward really well and intimately. He loved to be involved with the smallest domestic details of the preliminary arrangements of the competition as well as the grand overall design. He was a vice-president of the organising committee. Vice-presidencies are usually thought of as merely honorific but he regularly attended our meetings. He would take a seat at the end of the table, having arrived at the last moment. Listening carefully to the discussions, he would skilfully intervene at a carefully timed moment (later rather than sooner) in order to make the greatest impact with the points he wished to emphasise. The impressions he gave at these meetings was that he valued and esteemed the opinions of each member of the committee. He enjoyed many of the peripheral tasks of the activities of the organisation. Thus, he undertook to write programme notes for fund-raising recitals, and it was during his period as chairman that we cemented our relationship with our sponsors, Harveys of Bristol, his support at this time being extremely valuable. On another occasion when Nadia Boulanger, at that time one of the most respected and revered musicians in the world, arrived at Leeds City station to serve on the 1972 jury, she telephoned me in consternation and not a little indignation to say that she had arrived at the station but there had been no-one there to welcome her. I rang Edward about this slip-up and he immediately took a taxi to the hotel and greeted her personally.

He realised that the social side is a very important aspect of our competition, which depends so much on voluntary help and financial donors. Edward was most appreciative of their help and never missed an opportunity of thanking them both privately and publicly. He made a point of thanking the ladies in the kitchen after our meals at the University.

Snobbery and pomposity irritated him and he would often be seen deep in conversation during a concert interval with a young musician rather than making small talk with a local dignitary.

One of the most arduous tasks of the competition is to choose the repertoire. Edward, Geoffrey and I would get together at weekends to select works which would have certain points of comparison as far as emotional content, length, technical difficulty and style were concerned. Our joint knowledge of the piano literature, adding to and subtracting from each other's suggestions, gave us hours of great pleasure until the final selection was made. His great sensitivity in personal relationships even made divergence of opinion enjoyable. During these discussions, he and Geoffrey would use their fine memories to suggest works with comparable lengths of timings so that each competitor would have similar lengths of programme to prepare. He insisted on being a voting chairman and also having, if required, a casting vote.

Edward confessed that he could not play the piano fluently but during his 'vacation weeks' in August before the start of the competition in September he spent many hours studying the scores of the pieces in the prescribed repertoire and listening to as many different recordings as he could find of each work. No one knew the scores better than he. He adored the music of Bach. Like the rest of the members of the jury he was very disappointed that so few competitors included any of the Bach set works in their programmes. Rosalyn Tureck, a great Bach exponent, was a jury member in 1975 and maybe her presence inhibited the competitors, as there are so many diverse opinions regarding the interpretation of his keyboard music. Should the pianist try to imitate the tone and timbre of the eighteenth-century harpsichord and clavichord or should he exploit to the full the varied sonorities of the modern Steinway concert grand? Little did any of us realise that year that Andras Schiff, who came third, would become an authority on the performance of Bach's keyboard music. However, it would be as unfair to label Schiff as a Bach specialist only as it would to regard Murray Perahia as 'the great Mozartian' only. They and our other most celebrated prize-winners give performances and record with equal distinction most of the great composers from Bach to Bartok.

Edward disliked using the bell to stop a competitor who was overrunning his allotted time and he resisted the prods and upturned eyes of other members of the jury when they felt that a competitor's performance might well be curtailed. In fact, the more mediocre the performance, the more meticulous Edward was in allowing the full measure of time. However, I do remember him running out of patience at the end of a day when we had heard 11 performances of the third Prokofiev Sonata, seven of them in succession and he remarked, 'I do not think that I ever want to hear that work again!'

He was as well aware as I was that we were looking for young pianists with a touch that would proclaim mastery; not only with fine techniques but also beauty of tone, musical understanding and integrity, rhythmic vitality and, above all, that indefinable inspiration that defies analysis and makes the listener *listen*.

Being chairman of an international music jury is onerous and carries with it a great responsibility not only to the competitors but also to the donors of engagements and the public. After the excitement and razzmatazz of the competition has died down these are the people who are guided by the final judgements of the jury and will set the seal of approval or, indeed, disapproval on their decisions.

Edward used to refer to himself simply as a music lover. However, after the first few days of the fourth competition in 1972, Nadia Boulanger took me aside and said, 'Miss Waterman, I want to ask you a very personal question. Who is Edward Boyle?' At first I was taken aback by this question, but then I told her of his past and present achievements and offices. 'But,' she exclaimed, 'he is a great musician!' And this was the impression he made on all his musical colleagues. They loved and respected him because of his great knowledge, manifest fairness and integrity.

The choice of members of the jury was always left in my hands and Edward was chairman of the jury in 1972, 1975 and 1978. These juries included among their members Artur Balsam (USA), Nadia Boulanger (France), Halina Czerny-Stefanska (Poland), Ingrid Haebler (Austria) and Dmitri Bashkirov (USSR), to name but a few of the internationally renowned musicians. These musicians from all corners of the world, with their different cultures, nationalities and languages, have to live and work together day after day for up to ten hours a day under stressful conditions with very little time for relaxation or refreshment.

Edward had a flair for uniting everyone in friendship and there was rarely a discordant note. He skilfully handled a potentially difficult and volatile group of musical personalities and, without suppressing their individual characters, allowed them to form their own opinions independently. His own judgements were based on knowledge, experience, common sense, kindness and an inborn integrity.

One of the most poignant moments in the Leeds Competition is when the jury go to Tetley Hall (the university hall of residence where the competitors stay) for the chairman to announce to the waiting and agitated competitors the names of those who are to go forward to the next stage. Those fortunate enough to be named leave the room to discuss with the organisation their practising arrangements for the forthcoming round. The unfortunate ones remain behind and having, in some cases, composed themselves, discuss with each member of the jury in turn points of their interpretations and impressions about their performances, the jurors referring to the notes they have made. Edward was unique. He made hardly a note, trusting his almost infallible memory to recall their performances and interpretations in the minutest detail; for example, he remembered their different tempi, moods, tone, rubato and dynamics and also whether repeats had been made and how they varied from the original statement of a theme. He was never in a hurry and, glass of wine in hand, he would stay talking to them until he had spoken to each one in turn, offering advice, comfort and encouragement. I recall one member of the jury earnestly discussing the performance of the first movement of the Appassionata Sonata with a competitor. 'But,' the young man replied, 'I didn't play the Appassionata, I played the Waldstein.' This could never have happened to Edward Boyle.

We had many discussions on the advantages and disadvantages of musical competitions but Edward had become a great supporter of the Leeds Competition after hearing Radu Lupu's performance of Beethoven's third Piano Concerto on television in 1969. 'Why', he wondered, 'should a fine artist like Radu Lupu have to enter another competition having won first prize at the Van Cliburn Competition three years previously?' Edward realised that the large number of prestigious national and international engagements offered to our competition helped a young artist on the brink of a career much more than a large cash prize. He did not foresee that in another three years he himself would be involved in the launching of another great artist. He was so proud to have been chairman of the jury in 1972, when Murray Perahia, now acknowledged to be one of the greatest pianists of our time, won first prize. There was mutual admiration, respect and affection between them.

He also followed the careers of several of the other prize-winners such as Mitsuko Uchida and Andras Schiff by attending their concerts in London and the provinces. Dimitri Alexeev, first prize-winner in 1975, whose career in England was affected by the political tensions between East and West, was a particular favourite of his and he took every opportunity of saying that Alexeev's playing was consequently much underestimated by the general musical public.

News of Edward's grievous illness came from him in a personal and confidential letter to Geoffrey of 20 November 1979:

> I have been given *every* encouragement to think optimistically about the future, in terms of years not months – clearly I'll be a health risk, but I'm *not* going to retire into my shell – only give up certain things like overnight travel. I plan to keep plenty of reserves for next autumn's competition.[1]

Listening to music with Edward was an experience and we were never happier than when we were sharing our musical experiences together. There was, however, a moving occasion one wintry night when we fetched him from the Vice-Chancellor's Lodge to listen to Benjamin Frith[2] playing the Hammerklavier Sonata. After fifty minutes of intense listening to this fine young pianist, there was an equally intense silence and to break this highly charged moment, I suggested listening to a recording of Schubert's Die Winterreise performed by Peter Pears and Benjamin Britten. It was an apt but perhaps unhappy choice because at this time Edward's final illness was already upon him. I think that this was the only time I ever saw tears in his eyes.

In a letter dated 15 June 1981, he writes, 'I have written to Murray, confirming 11 a.m. next Sunday the 21st, and of course I hope you will be able to join us here as well.' This was a sad and significant meeting because it was as a result of this that Edward asked Murray Perahia to play the second movement of the Schubert G major Sonata at his Memorial Service in the University.

During one of our regular visits to him in hospital in August 1981 he said to me, 'This is one of the saddest moments of my life. I feel I cannot undertake the chairmanship of the jury next month and would like you to take my place.' It was also a very sad moment for me as I realised then that he had given up.

His letters were always worth reading because one always learnt something new. On 20 April 1980:

> As for last night's concert, it was memorable – but I enjoyed Vanya's[3] performance by far the most of all. I've always loved the E major slow movement of K 219 ever since I first heard it as a boy (played with a piano accompaniment in our sitting-room at home), and I've never heard it played with such beautiful classical poise as last night. I only wish we could have had the alternative slow movement Mozart composed for Brunetti – K 261 – played as an encore before the interval! You must have felt *very* proud.

On 1 February 1978 in another illuminating letter:

> I never open a score of great music without a fresh sense of wonder. Just imagine what it must have felt like for Beethoven to have decided to scrap the *andante favori* as the slow movement of the Waldstein Sonata – a beautiful enough movement in all conscience and to replace it with that daring *introduzione* which couldn't hope to command so instant an appeal, and of which he himself had to make six sketches. There are no people in history who command my deeper admiration than the greatest composers.

It was always a privilege to be in Edward's presence and to listen to his mellifluous voice expressing his innermost musical thoughts. How gently he treated us all in spite of that staggering intellect – one could not help feeling humble in his presence.

The competition was so dear to his heart and his involvement in it so important a refreshment to his life that he left a considerable sum in his will for the furtherance of its aims.

Remembering him now, I think of his magisterial figure, bonhomous and kindly, his pawky sense of humour (never at anyone's expense), his passion for music and his utter kindness and consideration at all times. Perhaps I was one of the privileged few with whom he lost his shyness and became an accessible, confiding and affectionate friend.

Notes

1. The Leeds National Competition for Musicians, November 1980. EB could only attend the final concert but made a magnificent speech from the platform.
2. Joint winner of the sixth Arthur Rubinstein International Piano Masters Competition, 1989.
3. Vanya Milanova, violinist. In fact Vanya Milanova played the Mozart Adagio in E, K 261 at the Royal Opera House Concert in aid of the Edward Boyle Memorial Trust on 6 February 1983.

20

The Benevolent Uncle
Georgina Dunlop

When we came out of the memorial service at St Margaret's Westminster, my brother Jason pointed out what he felt was a significant omission in Mr Heath's fine summary of our uncle Edward's life. Why had he not mentioned how Edward would, when really delighted, stand laughing with his hands in his pockets, rattling the loose change? It seemed a flippant point but the truth of it grew on me. It was Edward's extraordinary enthusiasm, his real delight in an amazingly wide range of subjects, that made him unique.

He was kind enough to enjoy coming to the circus with me when I took a group there at about the age of eight; he was delighted to hear that Jason was studying Wittgenstein at Sussex University as part of his logic course, saying with obvious pleasure that Wittgenstein was perhaps the hardest to understand of all philosophers; he would quote P. G. Wodehouse with glee; he took an interest in cricket, remembering statistics with amazing accuracy; he loved gardening, knowing the names of all the daffodils in his garden, sometimes also mentioning the names of their parents; his greatest pleasure was music, and he had an incredible memory for details of performances. He loved the family life he had with us; and he once mentioned that as Minister of Education one thing he really enjoyed was going in to work on a Monday morning and finding that some really difficult problems had arrived on his desk.

He remained a bachelor and we were the closest part of his family – my parents, Ann and Jack Gold, my brother Jason, two years older than me, and myself. On Sunday evenings the telephone would regularly ring at nine and I would sit at my bedroom door listening to my mother relaying our week's activities and then receiving his rather more significant news.

The first time I heard him speak in public, at a Handsworth Ladies' Fashion Show, I was enchanted. He had a wonderfully friendly and intimate way of speaking; it was as though he were addressing his remarks to you personally, and his tone was almost conversational. If he made a quotation from some erudite work, it seemed to be understood that you were of course familiar with it. This could sometimes be disconcerting in conversation; I often found it hard to look intelligent as he quoted someone I had not even heard of, and he sometimes found it slightly exasperating if one looked totally ignorant.

We would spend several days of the Easter and Christmas school holidays, and at least a week in summer, at the Boyle country house, Ockham. In summer he would come by car to collect us from Westgate-on-Sea where we had been staying. He would arrive for lunch with us at our seaside hotel, and in the afternoon play with us on the beach, very skilful at digging networks of canals in the sand. He loved the drive through the pretty Kent villages, taking the most direct route back to Ockham, having chosen a different way to come to meet us.

To me Ockham was magical. Very little had been altered since the war; the last significant changes had been made in the 1930s, by my grandmother, who had enjoyed putting some finishing touches, like decorating and equipping a little room for serving cocktails – very elegant details.

The house had great opportunities for hide-and-seek and for running its great length on the first floor, with only one swing door halfway along to interrupt one's journey. I'm not sure how tiresome we were but there was never a hint of criticism from Edward. He always seemed pleased to see that we were enjoying ourselves. There was even a large toy cupboard next to my bedroom, and although most of the toys were not very exciting it was always a treat to investigate it. My favourites were a dozen pre-war Pip and Squeak annuals. Edward would apologise for the oldness of the toys but in fact this gave them added charm. Sometimes we played in his study, still known as the day nursery because of its original use, which was next to Jason's and my bedrooms, full of books and often also ministerial papers – sometimes we would try to read these but they always seemed terribly dull. On top of one small bookcase were three items: a fretwork cut-out photograph of my grandfather, Edward's father; a photograph of the elderly Brahms; and a framed quotation:

> I expect to pass through this world but once; any good thing therefore that I can do, or any kindness that I can show to any

fellow-creature let me do it now; let me not defer or neglect it, for I shall not pass this way again.[1]

These three things always seemed to me as a child to define Edward's character, although in fact I believe it was not he who had put them there. It was not at all his style to change things, however, so there they stayed.

The 'big room' was the main sitting-room, about 20 feet by 40 feet, with a minstrel's gallery at one end, and two storeys high. The curtains and carpet were red and in winter the log fire was burning from teatime to bedtime. We had dinner in the lovely oak-panelled dining-room, with candlelight making the silver candlesticks sparkle; and after dinner Edward always played us music in the big room. He had a vast record collection, and of course knew every performance in detail. He always gave us the libretto to follow if it was a vocal work, or the record sleeve to read to find out about the piece.

A large lawn stretched out behind the house, with a beautiful view of the rolling Sussex hills. The rest of the garden was laid out in sections: the 'wild garden', the rose garden, the 'Dutch garden' containing bulbs, and so on. In spring, the 'wild garden' was full of daffodils and narcissi – Edward loved to take us round, naming every flower; in summer the roses were glorious; in winter sometimes it would snow and we would have marvellous sledging on the hill at the front of the house.

Jason had an 8 mm movie camera and one of the things we did at Ockham was make films. I must have been about 11 and Jason 13 when Edward very sportingly agreed to appear in 'The Case', a detective thriller about a murderer (me) who roamed the gardens at Ockham killing anyone she met by spraying them with 'crazy foam', delightful stuff that came out of an aerosol can. Edward laughed and laughed when he later saw himself on screen, sinking very cautiously to the ground with white foam on his suit, and he good-naturedly apologised for his undramatic performance.

He was always interested in the things Jason and I enjoyed. He joined us to watch a television programme which we told him was important about the greatest pop group of the day, Blind Faith. Edward rattled the change in his pockets with delight as Jack Bruce stated that of course Bach was the original King of the Blues. He asked our advice on adding a couple of representative pop records to his vast classical collection, and on our recommendation he bought LPs by Cream and the Rolling Stones.

Jason told us that it was the custom at his junior school, in response to praise from the master, to flap the lapels of one's blazer to cool one's modest blushes, murmuring, 'fans, fans.' Edward later reported that Mr Macmillan had accepted one of his proposals at a Cabinet meeting by replying, 'I think that's a very good suggestion, Edward,' and so, Edward explained to Jason, he had not spoken but had gently moved the lapels of his coat.

I was at times rather cheeky as a little girl, although I always tried to be on my best behaviour with him. 'Naughty child,' he would say with great delight if my manners did slip; usually it was 'darling child.'

Edward was always very encouraging to us and interested to know how we were getting on at school, without our feeling at all pressured. When I had disappointing results in my 'A' levels, he immediately started considering what options were open to me, and asked the principal of Homerton teacher training college at Cambridge, whom he knew, whether I might be a suitable student. However, he was sensitive enough to know I was better left to come to my own decision and he said nothing of it to me. My mother casually mentioned the idea to me some weeks later, and it then seemed excellent. He kindly gave me an allowance while I was there, mentioning that he would like to think that it would be spent mostly on books. There was also the occasional cheque at other times for something special, as well as at birthdays and Christmas.

Carlton Club
69 St James's Street, SW1
10.11.78

Dearest Georgina,
   Many happy returns – and I'm sorry this is late. I am enclosing a contribution to the cost of your trip to Turkey, which I am sure you will enjoy very much. I once went to Istanbul, for a meeting of the World Bank and the IMF, and greatly enjoyed the 'sights'. Don't miss the Blue Mosque, or Santa Sophia of course; and there are fine frescoes in the Kurie church; I remember that, while I was admiring them, Lord Butler read a cross letter from Anthony Eden saying that his health was quite all right, and that there was no need for Butler to come back early as he had proposed.
   Much love,

   Edward

After he sold Ockham, he would always spend Christmas Day with us at our home in London. He would generously return our hospitality by giving us dinner at the Connaught Hotel soon after Christmas, and he also took us there at the end of August to celebrate his and my father's birthdays. Once we actually went somewhere else but it did not seem nearly so pleasant and thereafter we always stuck to the Connaught – he much preferred always doing the same thing. Choosing a present for him was always terribly difficult, as he was a classic 'man who has everything'. If I had gone abroad on holiday I would always try to bring something back for him, as it would give it slightly more point. Whatever it was, his face would light up with pleasure and he would give the most delightful little speech of thanks making the present seem quite perfect.

The other regular treat that he gave us was the opera at Glyndebourne, perhaps his greatest pleasure, and certainly mine. We had a delightful routine, dinner in the restaurant during the interval followed by a walk through the garden. We always took the same route, out of the opera house at the side, through the White Garden, across the lawn and back through the drawing room. Once by chance we met him there earlier than usual, and, feeling almost guilty, we took a walk we had not done before – to the end of the lake.

In 1981, I chose the occasion of dinner at Glyndebourne, as we were all together – both my parents and Edward – to announce that I was going to get married. I asked Edward to choose the music for the wedding. He used his extensive record collection to help him make the decisions, and he was even kind enough to travel to London in July to come with us to see the church organist. Edward had only two months to live, and my fiancé was stunned that someone who was by now extremely frail could still remember even the bar numbers of the music, especially after waiting uncomfortably without a word of complaint for the organist, who was very late.

It must have been an exhausting day for him as it was later that same day that my mother and I drove him to see Jason and his wife's new baby, Matthew, Edward's first great-nephew. Edward asked to hold the baby for a while.

He survived by sheer determination to come to my wedding in September, although his doctor told him a day or two before the wedding that he would not be able to manage even the journey. But Edward would not accept his doctor's judgement or his own frailty and the ambulance was ordered to take him to London, where he stayed in a nursing home. At the ceremony his wheelchair was put next to my mother by the front pew and when I started to walk up the aisle I was amazed to see that he was standing up, with my mother's help. My nervousness as I arrived at the altar evaporated as I heard his voice saying firmly, 'No,' and I guessed it was in response to my mother asking if he would rather sit down now. He was determined to do the whole thing properly and not sit until the rest of the congregation did so.

At the reception, my godmother had been asked to give the speech proposing the health of the bride and bridegroom, since it had seemed clear for some time that Edward would not be able to do so. Our best man decided that we should revert to the original plan; he went over to Edward's chair and asked him to give the speech. Edward was very reluctant, saying he was unprepared, but John insisted, and the result was spooky. Edward rose unaided to his feet, and it was as if five years fell away. Saying that he had not expected to give the speech he went on, 'I'd just like to say three things . . . ' and it was as if the speech had taken spontaneous form in his mind as the themes (I forget what they were, I was so amazed) expanded like a perfect Bacon essay. We were going to have a two-week honeymoon and I told John I felt uncomfortable being away for so long. 'He'll probably live another five years,' John said.

In fact he lived another three weeks, and I returned from my honeymoon just in time to join my mother in Leeds for a final weekend.

Note

1. Attributed to Stephen Grellet, 1773–1855.

Index

Abinger Hill preparatory school 8–10, 55–7, 86, 90, 158
Albania 48
Alexeev, Dimitri 171
Amery, Julian 70, 72
Amory, Derick Heathcoat 27
Ampleforth College 51
Anderson, Sir John 64
Anderson Committee 98
Anglo-Catholic church 17
Any Questions 91
d'Aranyi, Jelly 50, 150
Armstrong, Sir Thomas 18, 159
Arts Council 33
Astor, David 51
Astor, J.J. 62
Athanaeum Club 116
Atkinson, Frederick 88
Attlee, Lord 71

Bach, J.S. 168
Balkan Committee, The 4
Bayley, John 65
Beethoven, L. van 163
Beefsteak Club 116
Benn, Tony 19, 21, 120
Birch, Nigel 23
Birmingham Unionist Association 20
Bletchley Park 15–16
Boulanger, Nadia 168, 169, 170
Boyle, Beatrice (mother) 5–6, 27, 48, 114, 158
Boyle, Constance (grandmother) 1, 7, 15, 16
Boyle, Sir Edward (grandfather) 2, 4
Boyle, Sir Edward (father) 2–5, 8–9, 13–14, 15, 16, 63
Boyle, Sir Edward Charles Gurney, Lord Boyle of Handsworth
childhood 1–6
schooldays *see* Abinger Hill school and Eton College
war work *see* Bletchley Park
military training 13–14
university *see* Oxford University
assistant editor, *National Review* 65–8
elected to Parliament 21 *see also* Handsworth
at Ministry of Supply 23
appointed to the Treasury 24 *see also* Economic Secretary and Financial Secretary
resigns from the government 25 *see also* Suez crisis
returns to the government 25–6 *see also* Education
opposition front-bench spokesman 30
 see also Education
speaking style 61, 107, 174–5
retires from the House of Commons 35, 112
appointed Vice-Chancellor 35

Index

see also Leeds University illness and death 4–45
Boyle, Sir Richard Gurney (brother) 8, 27
Bramall, Field-Marshal Lord (Edwin) 73
Brahms, Johannes 161, 162, 165, 175
Bridges, Sir Edward 85–6
British Museum trustees 48, 116
Britten, Benjamin 161
Brown, Shelagh 96
Browning, Robert 54
Bunyan, John 142
Burnham Committee 28
Butler, R.A. 28, 35, 39, 53, 69, 85–6, 87, 92, 121, 122, 123, 177

Campbell-Bannerman, Sir Henry 3
Carlton Club, 27, 116
Carr, Robert 93
Carr-Saunders Memorial Lecture 75, 144
Chamberlain, Mrs Neville 20
Christopherson, Sir Derman 130
Churchill, Sir Winston 23, 64, 68, 70
Civil Service see Fulton Committee
Clark, Charles 31
Collingwood, R.J. 57
Committee of Vice-Chancellors and Principals 38–9, 137
Companion of Honour 44
Comprehensive schools see Education
Coningsby Club 138
Connaught Hotel 114, 178
Cricket 11, 49, 73–4, 77–8

Crosland, Anthony 67, 88, 97, 99, 108, 120
Curriculum Study Group 98
Czechoslovakia 34

Death penalty, abolition of 82
de Keyser, Geoffrey 168, 171
Department of Education and Science see Education
Ditchley Foundation 116
Dream of Gerontius 17–18
Douglas-Home, Sir Alec see Home, Lord
Dykes, Rev. J.B. 13

Economic Secretary to Treasury 24–5, 50, 69, 85–8, 92, 121
Eden, Sir Anthony 25, 51, 60, 64, 69, 70-1, 93, 95, 113, 177
Education
Parliamentary Secretary 26–7, 52, 95–6, 100–1
  Minister of Education, 27, 96–103, 104–12, 115
  formation of Dept. of Education and Science 29, 111
  Minister of State, DES 29
  comprehensive schools 108–10, 122, 164
  debate on teachers' salaries 28
  opposition spokesman for education 30, 78
  raising of the school-leaving age 29, 99, 115
  special educational needs of immigrant children 75
  teacher supply 100
  thoughts on education and higher education
Eliot, T.S. 156

Elliot, Claude 61
Eton College 10, 11–13, 59–62, 73–4, 91
European University Institute 42

Fachiri, Adila 50, 158
Fair Cricket campaign 77
Fauré, Gabriel 43, 118, 161, 162, 163, 165, 166
Fellowes, Edward 92
Financial Secretary to the Treasury 27
Fletcher, Ralph 96
Frith, Benjamin 171
Fulton Committee 33, 89–90
Fulton, Lord 39

Gaitskell, Hugh 67, 86
Gedalge, André 159
Gervais, Françoise 161
Gittins Committee 98
Gladstone, W.E. 123
Glock, Sir William 167
Glyndebourne 34, 93, 178
Gold, Ann (sister) 6, 50, 125, 174
Gold, Georgina (*later* Dunlop) 45, 50
Gold, Jack 50, 174
Gold, Jason 174, 176, 177, 178
Gregynog lectures 144
Greig, Henry 5
Grigg, Sir Edward 59, 65
Grigg, John 73

Hailsham, Lord (Quintin Hogg) 26, 29, 100, 111, 115
Hall, Robert 85, 86
Handsworth 21–2, 24, 25, 29–30, 74, 75, 89, 114, 117, 174

Harkness fellowships 34
Harris, Kenneth 81
Harrod, Roy 66
Harrogate music festival 43
Hayek, Friedrich 63, 88
Head, Ray 133
Heath, Edward 42, 46, 76, 122, 123, 132, 140
Henderson, Arthur 96
Henderson, Hubert 88, 93
Home, Lord (Sir Alec Douglas-Home) 28, 97, 111
Hopkins, Gerard Manley 145
House of Lords 39
Howard, Michael 101

Institute of Race Relations 33
Iliad, The 124

Jaffé, Michael
James, Henry 142
Junior Carlton club 139

Kaldor, Nicholas 88
Kent, HRH The Duchess of, 46

Lane, Sir Allen 31–32, 139
Leavis, R.R. and Q.D. 139, 142, 145
Leeds Grammar School 166
Leeds piano Competition 43, 45, 160, 166–73
Leeds University 34–5, 37–8, 72, 118, 123, 124–34, 135–7, 138–46
Legge, Walter 43
Ley, Henry 13, 159
Liddell Hart, Adrian 61
Lloyd, Geoffrey 20, 26, 97, 106, 121
Lloyd, Selwyn 27, 104, 111

Lupu, Radu 171

McCreath, Margaret
MacGregor, James 133
Macleod, Iain 94, 121, 123
Macmillan, Harold 28, 46, 69, 92, 93, 113, 122, 132
   invites E.B. to serve as his temporary PPS 23
   is appointed to the Treasury when E.B. is Economic Secretary 25
   invites E.B. to rejoin the government after Suez 25–6, 52–3, 71–2
   asks E.B. to draft a passage on West Indian cricket 78
   interviews a prospective junior Minister 104
McNair-Scott, Valerie 53
Magic Flute, The 158
Maudling, Reginald 121
May, Henry 5
Mays Memorial lecture 144
Mellers, Wilfred 146
Milanova, Vanya 172
Mill, John Stuart 102
Milner, Lord 45
Milner, Lady 65
Monckton, Sir Walter 113
Moore, Gerald 43, 160
Morrell, Derek 96
Morris, Lord 140
Mossadek, Dr. 70
Mozart, W.A. 166, 172

Nabarro, Sir Gerald 77
National Review (later *National and English Review*) 65–8, 70–1
Nectoux, J-M. 162

Nenk, David 96
Newsom Report 29, 99, 109
Nutting, Anthony 92–3
Oxford University
   E.B. wins history scholarship to Christ Church 11
   goes up to Oxford 17–18
   interest in church music and the High Church 18
   speaks at the Union 57, 65, 120
   goes on Union debating tour of USA 18, 81–2
   examination results 20, 58, 121
Oakeshott, Michael 145
Orledge, Robert 162

Pakenham, Thomas 51–2
Part, Antony 96
Pattison, Bruce 146
Pearson Commission 33
Peel, Sir Robert 123
Penguin Books 31–3
Perahia, Murray 46, 169, 171, 172
Perry Barr 19, 20
Pilgrim Trust 34, 116
Plowden Committee 98, 99
Popper, Karl 42–2, 102–3, 123
Positivism 5
Powell, Enoch 76, 77, 123
Pratt's Club 116

Quickswood, Lord 61

Race relations 30, 75–8, 93
Rawlinson, Sir Anthony 132
Reith lectures 43, 144
Richard Feetham Memorial

lecture 144
Robbins, Lionel 88
Robbins Report 28, 97, 99, 100, 111
Roberts, Harold 19, 21
Roberts, Margaret 120 *see also* Thatcher
Robertson, Dennis 88
Roll, Michael 166
Rose, Kenneth 65
Ross, Maureen 125
Routh, C.R.N. 10, 60
Royal Northern College of Music 157

Sandys, Duncan 23
Schiff, Andras 169, 171
Schools Council 98
Schwartzkopf, Elisabeth 43, 160
Scrutiny 145–6
Serbian Relief Fund 4
Shires, Harry 29
Smethwick parliamentary election 76
South African cricket tour 77
Spicer, Roger 61
Stevens, Sir Roger 37, 138
Suckling, Norman 162–3
Suez crisis and E.B.'s resignation 25, 51, 69–72, 74, 82–3, 88–9, 92–3, 113, 122, 139
Swanton, E.W. 74

Teacher supply 100
Templewood, Lord 101
Thatcher, Margaret (Margaret Roberts) 35, 42, 45, 122

The Times 79, 111, 153
Thorpe, Marion 167
Top Salaries Review Body 42, 83, 118, 147–54
Tovey, Sir Donald 155, 157
Treasury, The 85–9, 121–2 *see also* Economic Secretary
Trevor-Roper, Hugh 17
Truman, President 67
Tunbridge, Sir Ronald 138
Tureck, Rosalyn 168
Uchida, Mitsuko 171
UNESCO 26
United University Club 139
University Grants Committee 111

Wagner's school 1, 7–8
Walsh, James 133
Walker, Peter 106
Walsh, William 46
Waterman, Fanny 160
Watson, Steven 17, 19, 20
Weaver, Toby 96
Webb, Kaye 32
Wells, Sir Richard 63, 64
West Indian cricket: Weekes, Walcott and Worrell 78
Whitelaw, Lord 132
Wille, Professor Georg 6
Williams, Ruth (m. Seretse Khama) 49
Wilson, Harold 39, 42, 67, 111
Winston Churchill Memorial Trust 34
World Bank 24

Young, Hugo 97